PELICAN BOOKS

A 176

BIRD RECOGNITION

II

BIRDS OF PREY AND
WATER-FOWL

JAMES FISHER

JAMES FISHER

BIRD RECOGNITION

II

BIRDS OF PREY AND
WATER-FOWL

*

With 85 illustrations by
FISH-HAWK

82 maps compiled by
W. B. ALEXANDER

*and 71 charts compiled by the
writer*

PENGUIN BOOKS

HARMONDSWORTH . MIDDLESEX

First published 1951

FOR

Crispin

Made and printed in Great Britain
for Penguin Books Ltd
by Harrison & Sons Ltd, Printers to His Majesty the King

INTRODUCTION

THIS is the second of four volumes whose object is to enable bird-watchers to distinguish the different sorts of birds likely to be met with in the British Isles, and to recognise their place in nature and general importance. Volume I, on sea-birds and waders, has been widely distributed – there appears to be a very large number of observers of birds in Britain. Volume III, on rails, game-birds and larger perching and singing birds; and Volume IV on the smaller perching and singing birds, are to follow.

Bird Recognition attempts to provide a statement of the present status of the British birds, as well as of their recognition-points. As observers increase, and the numbers and habits of birds change (both these processes may be rapid), this book therefore becomes out-of-date. Already Vol. I has to be revised, and a new edition is being published. I hope that readers will tolerate the necessary intervals between new editions, and will continue to inform me of additions and corrections as they have been kind enough to do with Volume I.

I must once more thank my patient collaborators, 'Fish-Hawk' (David Wolfe-Murray) and W. B. Alexander. Peter Scott has given me very helpful advice about the ducks and geese in this volume, and I thank him too.

I must refer the reader to pp. 5–14 of Vol. I for an explanation of the general system, a list of books on bird recognition, a key vice-county list and map, an explanation of the year-cycle charts and a diagram of the externals of a bird. The numbers at the bottom of the text-pages, prefixed by the letter W, correspond to those in the check-list in Witherby's *Handbook*, the standard textbook of British birds.

	At Sea	Rocky Coasts	Estuaries and Dunes	Marshes and Inland Waters	Mountains, Moors and Heaths	Wood- and Parkland	Farm-, Grassland and Hedges	Towns and Buildings
WHITE-TAILED EAGLE	■	■		■	■			
OSPREY		■		■				
MERLIN		■	■		■		■	
GOLDEN EAGLE			■		■			
COMMON BUZZARD			■		■	■		
GYR-FALCON			■		■			
PEREGRINE			■		■		■	
KESTREL			■		■	■	■	
LITTLE OWL			■		■	■	■	
SNOWY OWL			■	■	■			
ROUGH-LEGGED BUZZARD				■	■		■	
MONTAGU'S HARRIER			■	■	■		■	
SHORT-EARED OWL			■	■	■		■	
HEN-HARRIER			■	■	■		■	
LONG-EARED OWL				■	■	■		
MARSH-HARRIER				■			■	
KITE						■	■	
HOBBY						■	■	
BARN-OWL							■	■
GOSHAWK						■		
HONEY-BUZZARD						■	■	
SPARROW-HAWK						■	■	
TAWNY OWL						■	■	■
	At Sea	Rocky Coasts	Estuaries and Dunes	Marshes and Inland Waters	Mountains, Moors and Heaths	Wood- and Parkland	Farm-, Grassland and Hedges	Towns and Buildings

	At Sea	Rocky Shores	Estuaries, Lagoons and Flats	Large Fresh Lakes and Open Waters	Rivers and Streams	Small Lakes and Reedy Meres	Marshes, Boggy Pools and Sewage-Farms	Water-Meadows, Flood-land and Grassland	Cornland	Town Waters	Woodland and Park-land
LONG-TAILED DUCK	■	■	■								
EIDER	■	■	■								
VELVET-SCOTER	■	■	■								
SURF-SCOTER	■	■	■								
SCOTER	■	■	■								
BRENT GOOSE	■	■	■								
BARNACLE-GOOSE		■	■					■			
SHELDUCK		■	■								
RED-BREASTED MERGANSER	■	■	■								
SCAUP	■	■	■								
PINTAIL			■	■		■	■				
GOOSANDER			■	■	■	■					
GOLDENEYE			■	■	■	■					
WIGEON			■	■		■	■	■			
POCHARD			■	■		■	■			■	
WHOOPER SWAN			■	■		■	■	■			
BEWICK'S SWAN			■	■		■	■	■			
SMEW			■	■	■	■					
BEAN-GOOSE			■			■	■	■			
PINK-FOOT			■			■	■	■	■		
WHITE-FRONT			■			■	■	■	■		
GREY-LAG			■			■	■	■	■		
MUTE SWAN			■	■	■	■	■	■		■	
MALLARD			■	■	■	■	■	■	■	■	■
CANADA GOOSE			■		■		■	■		■	■
TUFTED DUCK			■	■		■	■			■	
GADWALL			■	■		■	■				
TEAL			■			■	■	■			
SHOVELER			■			■	■	■			
FERRUGINOUS DUCK			■	■		■	■				
GARGANEY						■	■	■			

	At Sea	Coastal Waters	Large Fresh Lakes and Open Waters	Rivers and Streams	Small Lakes and Reedy Meres	Marshes, Boggy Pools and Sewage-Farms	Water-Meadows and Floodland	Towns	Grass- and Arable Land	Woodland
RED-NECKED GREBE	■	■	■							
GREAT NORTHERN DIVER	■	■	■							
BLACK-THROATED DIVER	■	■	■							
RED-THROATED DIVER	■	■	■							
GREAT CRESTED GREBE	■	■	■	■	■					
SPOONBILL		■		■	■	■				
SLAVONIAN GREBE		■	■	■	■					
BLACK-NECKED GREBE		■	■	■	■	■				
DABCHICK			■	■	■	■				
*COOT			■	■	■	■			■	
HERON				■	■	■	■	■	■	■
*MOORHEN				■	■	■	■	■	■	■
LITTLE BITTERN					■	■				
BITTERN					■	■				
*SPOTTED CRAKE					■	■	■			
*LITTLE CRAKE					■	■	■			
*BAILLON'S CRAKE					■	■	■			
*WATER-RAIL					■	■	■			
NIGHT-HERON						■	■			■
STORK						■	■		■	
*CORN-CRAKE									■	■

| | At Sea | Coastal Waters | Large Fresh Lakes and Open Waters | Rivers and Streams | Small Lakes and Reedy Meres | Marshes, Boggy Pools and Sewage-Farms | Water-Meadows and Floodland | Towns | Grass- and Arable Land | Woodland |

* Described in Volume III.

FIELD CHARACTER KEYS

The use of these keys is explained in Vol. I, pp. 15–16. The precise meanings of the words for size are as follows:—

Adjective	Length in inches	Example
Small	8–12	Little owl
Small-medium	12–16	Sparrow-hawk
Medium	16–20	Wigeon
Medium-large	20–24	Mallard
Large	24–28	Great northern diver
Very large	28–32	Grey-lag
Immense	32–36	Golden eagle
Gigantic	over 36	Mute swan

There are no very small (length 6–8 inches), minute (5–6 inches), very minute (4–5 inches), or tiny birds (under 4 inches) mentioned in this volume.

FIELD CHARACTER KEY TO BRITISH OWLS

1. *a.* Medium-large; quite white with some brown bars; diurnal; haunts open country; flight like buzzard's
   SNOWY OWL (p. 26)

   b. Small-medium; flight silent with slow wing-beats .. see 2

   c. Small; plump; flat 'frowning' head; grey-brown upper parts flecked whitish, whitish under-parts streaked dark; can be diurnal; flight like woodpecker's................
   LITTLE OWL (p. 28)

2. *a.* Orange-buff upper-parts; pure white, or lightish, face and under-parts; pale and ghostly; can be diurnal.........
   BARN-OWL (p. 36)

   b. Brownish................................... see 3

3. *a.* Diurnal; open country away from trees; very long narrow wings, somewhat pointed; under-parts streaked but not barred .... SHORT-EARED OWL (p. 32)

   b. Nocturnal; usually woodland; shorter, broader, less pointed wings; under-parts streaked and barred...see 4

4. *a.* Smaller than *b.* Yellow eyes. Prominent ear-tufts, but as usually laid flat not often visible; greyer than short-eared owl; wings and tail shorter than short-eared owl's, but

9

longer than *b*'s. Upper-parts grey-buff and brown, under-parts have fairly well-marked transverse bars; slender upright stance.......... LONG-EARED OWL (p. 30)

b. Larger than *a.* Black eyes. No ear-tufts; rufous brown; broad short rounded wings; under-parts have faint bars; dumpy stance................ TAWNY OWL (p. 34)

FIELD CHARACTER KEY TO OTHER BRITISH BIRDS OF PREY

1. *a.* Interceptor type. Small to medium-large. Mostly active, direct, swift pursuit fliers: wings relatively short: hawks and falcons....................................see 2

   b. Prospector type. Medium to immense. Though some can fly swiftly and direct, all can soar or flap slowly: wings relatively long: eagles, buzzards, kite, harriers and osprey see 7

2. *a.* Pointed wings; relatively short tail; pursue prey in open; shortish legs: falcons..........................see 3

   b. Broad rounded wings: relatively long tail; can hunt prey with great agility through thick woodland or closed country: longish legs: hawks.....................see 6

3. FALCONS

a. Medium or medium-large: typically prey on game-birds and pigeons: stoop with astonishing power ......see 4

b. Small or small-medium: typically prey on small birds and mice: stoop with dexterity......................see 5

4. *a.* Medium-large. Relatively long tail. Relatively uniform colour; pale in all forms, white in some. 'Moustache' not well marked. Wings broader and blunter than *b*, and wing-beats slower..............GYR-FALCON (p. 38)

   b. Medium. Relatively short, tapering tail. Upper-parts dark blue-grey, under-parts buff-white barred black. 'Moustache' black, and black crown and sides of head. Wings long, sharply pointed. Rapid beats between long glides (see also 6*b*)..................... PEREGRINE (p. 40)

5. *a.* Extremely agile: small-medium; wings long, almost like those of swifts, comparatively short tail. May prey on swifts and swallows. Red thighs and under-tail (except juveniles); prominent black 'moustache' HOBBY (p. 42)

b. Very agile; small: wings less narrow and pointed than *a*; flight direct, and hunts close to ground; rapid beats between glides: hunts meadow-pipits and other small birds. Tail longer than *a*; no 'moustache'..............
MERLIN (p. 44)

c. Less agile; small-medium: wings much as *b* but tail markedly longer still; hovers perpetually and drops onto mice and voles. 'Moustache' not well-marked (see also 6*a*)
KESTREL (p. 46)

6. HAWKS

a. Small-medium. Barred, not streaked underparts and way of hunting distinguishes from kestrel, 5*c*. Male has dark slate-grey upper-parts, and rufous under-parts, no white eyestripe; female has browner upper-parts, whitish under-parts, and whitish eyestripe; bigger than male ....
SPARROW-HAWK (p. 60)

b. Medium-large. Plumage very much like female sparrow-hawk, 6*a*; size quite different. *Can* be confused with peregrine, 4*b*, in open flight but tail much longer, and often spread..................... GOSHAWK (p. 62)

7. *a.* Broad, rounded wings, not angled in soaring flight, leading edge at right-angles to axis of body..............see 8
b. Narrower, long wings, often angled.............see 12

8. *a.* Immense: head projects further in front of wings than *b*, and wings and tail are longer relative to body; tremendously powerful deliberate flight, and exceptionally strong bill: eagles ....see 9
b. Medium-large: majestic soaring flight: relative size does not prevent confusion with *a*: buzzards (see also 12*a*)....
see 10

9. EAGLES

a. Adult: dark tawny-brown plumage ; immature has white tail with broad black band at end. Tail longer and squarer than *b* ....GOLDEN EAGLE (p. 48)

b. Adult: head light; tail white; immature has brown tail. Tail shorter and more wedge-shaped than *a*. Wings broader and flight much more laboured; style more clumsy altogether .....WHITE-TAILED EAGLE (p. 66)

10. BUZZARDS, ETC.

a. Whole tail has narrow bars with broad bar near end: mewing note: walks clumsily on ground .... see 11

b. Tail has broad bars, more separated towards end: squeaky whistle: runs easily on ground: wings rather longer and narrower than *a*; head and neck extend further: under-parts more boldly patterned   HONEY-BUZZARD (p. 68)

11. *a.* Tail light, ends in broad dark band; usually whitish below: head light: heavier than *b*: legs feathered......
ROUGH-LEGGED BUZZARD (p. 50)

b. Tail dark: usually dark below: head dark: wings a little shorter than *a*: legs bare ..COMMON BUZZARD (p. 52)

12. *a.* Large: like buzzards (8*b*) but much longer, narrower and more angled wings. Very forked reddish tail: whitish patch under wing, towards end; under-parts pale red, dark streaks: head grey, streaked ....KITE (p. 64)

b. Medium-large: always near water, where drop-plunges for fish: dark brown above, white below (except light brown band across breast) and on head; wings long, narrow, angled; tail not very long, but narrow ....
OSPREY (p. 70)

c. Medium or medium-large: long wings, tail and legs; under-parts not white; haunt open country; hunt close to ground, glide between leisurely beats, harriers..see 13

13. HARRIERS

a. Medium-large. More rounded wings and heavier flight than *b*. Female and juvenile male has dark plumage, tail not barred. Male has brown upper parts, and tail and broad band across wing grey; black ends to wings......
MARSH-HARRIER (p. 54)

b. Medium. Obviously smaller than *a*, and more lightly built: wings narrower; less heavy in flight. Females have barred tails. Males have nearly uniform grey upper-parts and black wing-tips...........................see 14

14. *a.* (Male only.) Dark bar across secondary wing feathers (shows on underwing); rump grey; reddish streaks on flanks .,.............MONTAGU'S HARRIER (p. 56)

b. (Male only.) No wing-bar as *a*; large, conspicuous patch pure white on rump; no red on flanks................
HEN-HARRIER (p. 58)

Note. The hens and juvenile males of these species are very easily confused, and mistakes are likely. The Montagu's has longer and narrower wings and tail, is generally more slight, and has a narrower and less pure white patch at base of tail. The juveniles of Montagu's have plain, those of the hen-harrier streaked under-parts.

FIELD CHARACTER KEY TO BRITISH STORK AND HERONS

1. *a.* Fly with necks stretched out . . . . see 2
   b. Fly with necks retracted . . . . see 3

2. *a.* Immense; white, except most of wing and part of mantle black; long red legs and bill; bill straight, tapered sharp
   WHITE STORK (p. 72)
   b. Large; white; black legs and bill; bill long, spoon-shaped
   SPOONBILL (p. 74)
   c. Medium; brownish purple, often looks black; dark legs and bill; bill long, markedly downcurved . . . .
   GLOSSY IBIS (p. 76)

3. *a.* Mainly black and grey, with whitish under-parts . . . see 4
   b. Mainly brown and dark; nocturnal or crepuscular . . see 5

4. *a.* Very large; upper-parts and wings and tail grey; black band on white head extending back from eye to crest; diurnal . . . . HERON (p. 78)
   b. Medium-large; upper-parts mostly black, wings and tail grey; black crown; nocturnal . . . .
   ADULT NIGHT-HERON (p. 80)

5. *a.* Medium-large; under-parts grey with brown streaks; dark brown upper-parts boldly spotted with off-white . . . .
   YOUNG NIGHT-HERON (p. 80)
   b. Under-parts light brown streaked dark brown; upper-parts dark, or light streaked (not spotted) with dark . . see 6

6. *a.* Small-medium. Dark upper-parts and wing; rounded large light patch on wing (most marked in male) . . . .
   LITTLE BITTERN (p. 84)
   b. Large. Brown upper-parts and wings mottled and barred black; booms 'b'wump' . . . . BITTERN (p. 82)

13

FIELD CHARACTER KEY TO BRITISH SWANS, GEESE AND DUCKS

1. *a.* Plumage wholly white (young ash-brown); head and neck as long as body; gigantic..............SWANS; see 2
   b. Plumage in no case *wholly* white; though neck long, head and neck shorter than body GEESE AND DUCKS; see 4

2. SWANS

   a. Bill black and orange, black knob at base; swims with neck curved; relatively silent; length about 5 ft.........
   MUTE SWAN (p. 90)
   b. Bill black and yellow; swims with neck straight upright; relatively vocal ....see 3

3. *a.* Length about 5 ft.; yellow patch on bill tapers from base to a point below nostril; voice 'hoop-ah'..............
   WHOOPER SWAN (p. 86)
   b. Length about 4 ft.; forward boundary of yellow patch on bill is semicircle *behind* nostril; voice 'hoo'............
   BEWICK'S SWAN (p. 88)

4. *a.* Medium-large to gigantic; social, grazing, open-country, moor- and tundra-breeding birds; voice honking; sexes alike ....GEESE; see 5
   b. Small-medium to large; not all social; few grazing, breeding-habitat varied; voice quacking, whistling, grunting...........................DUCKS; see 11

5. GEESE

   a. Large or very large; general colour grey-brown; legs and feet and at least part of bill pink, flesh or orange; appearance of white tail with broad dark band near end......
   GREY GEESE; see 6
   b. Medium-large or immense; general colour dark; head and neck black marked with white; legs, feet, bill and tail black ....BLACK GEESE; see 9

6. GREY GEESE

   a. Black marks on breast, and bills with no black, and white 'nails' ....see 7 *b.* No black on breast, and bills with some black and black nails ....see 8

7. *a.* Very large; bill orange, large and stout, legs flesh; fore-wing pale grey; sometimes very narrow white 'front' above bill; breast *spotted* black; voice like farmyard goose....
GREY-LAG (p. 92)

b. Large; bill pink or yellow-pink, slighter than *a*'s, though robust; legs orange; fore-wing not paler than rest of wing; prominent white patch above bill; breast prominently *barred* black; the darkest of the grey geese; voice eerie dog-like laughing, high-pitched..................
ADULT WHITE-FRONT (p. 94)

8. *a.* Very large; bill orange-yellow and black, longer and heavier than that of other geese; legs orange or orange-yellow; fore-wing not paler than rest of wing; sometimes narrow white 'front' above bill; neck markedly long, not darker than back, but very dark head; white-edged feathers on mantle; the brownest of the grey geese; the most silent goose, voice like 8*b*'s only lower .BEAN-GOOSE (p. 96)

b. Large; bill black with pink band, small and fine; legs pink or pinkish-grey (yellowish in young); fore-wing *sometimes* paler than rest of wing; occasional trace of white 'front'; neck darker than back; voice intermediate between 7*a* and 7*b*........................ PINK-FOOT (p. 98)

c. Large; bill greyish-yellow; legs orange; fore-wing not paler than rest of wing; *no* white 'front' above bill, but dark feathering at its base; neck not darker than back; voice as 7*b*........ ....YOUNG WHITE-FRONT (p. 94)

9. BLACK GEESE

a. Medium-large; upper breast black; body mostly grey and white, wings grey and black; voice barking or croaking
see 10

b. Immense; upper breast, upper-parts, and wings brown, under-parts brown and white; white patch from chin to behind eye; voice trumpeting 'ah-'onk'................
CANADA GOOSE (p. 104)

10. *a.* Whole face and forehead white, with black mark from bill to eye; upper-parts grey narrowly barred black and white; under-parts pale grey; voice a series of yelping barks ....BARNACLE-GOOSE (p. 100)

b. Small white patch on sides of neck (none in juveniles); upper-parts slaty or brownish; under-parts slate-grey in dark-bellied race and whitish-grey in light-bellied race; voice 'ruk ... runk'.............BRENT GOOSE (p. 102)

11. DUCKS

a. Speculum resent. This is a patch, usually conspicuous, on the secondary wing-feathers which takes the form, as the duck floats or sits with folded wings, of a central parallelogram of some bright colour (often metallic) often bordered on each side by strips of a contrasting colour SHELDUCK (sexes alike) and SURFACE-FEEDING DUCKS (sexes unlike); see 12

b. No speculum, though often light patches or marks on wings; sexes unlike...................................
DIVING DUCKS AND SAW-BILLS; see 18

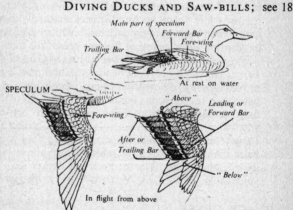

Main part of speculum

Forward Bar

Fore-wing

Trailing Bar

At rest on water

SPECULUM

"Above"

Leading or Forward Bar

Fore-wing

After or Trailing Bar

"Below"

In flight from above

12. *a.* Small-medium to medium-large. Sexes unlike (sober, 'browny' females). 'Duck-like' carriage and behaviour; relatively slender build; feed in shallow water mainly by dabbling and up-ending. Rise easily directly off water or land. Male goes into female-like plumage (eclipse) in summer. Bill and legs not red........................
SURFACE-FEEDING DUCKS; see 13

b. Medium-large. Sexes alike. 'Goose-like' carriage and behaviour; goose-like build; feeds on molluscs, etc., in shallow salt water. Unique pattern of black and chestnut on white, red bill (with knob) and pink feet............
SHELDUCK (p. 106)

13. SURFACE-FEEDING DUCKS

    a. Heads of males wholly dark green; belly not white; legs orange-red .... see 14

    b. Heads of males not wholly, if at all, green; belly white, or light, legs orange-yellow or grey .... see 15

14. *a.* (Both sexes.) Medium-large; bill 'duck-shaped' but not spoon-shaped; forewing brown, speculum purple, black above, white bars forward and aft.
(Male.) Belly grey; bill green-yellow; white collar below green of head; breast purple-brown; back grey.
(Female.) Belly and breast brown; bill dark olive, with orange at sides .... MALLARD (p. 108)

    b. (Both sexes.) Medium; bill huge and spoon-shaped; forewing blue; speculum green, with broad white bar forward and narrow white bar aft.
(Male.) Belly chestnut; bill black; no collar; breast white; back dark brown.
(Female.) Belly and breast brown and pink-buff; bill green-brown with yellow at sides and lower mandible dull orange
SHOVELER (p. 120)

15. *a.* Medium, or medium-large. Flight swift and straight, rapid wing-beats, with distinct whistling, hissing or fluttering noise, like mallard (14*a*); no eye-stripe .... see 16

    b. Small-medium. Flight swift and agile, may wheel like waders; wings nearly silent except when changing direction; males have eye-stripe .... see 17

16. *a.* (Both sexes.) Medium; head brown; forewing grey with chestnut patch; speculum white, dark below, broad black bar forward forms square white patch on trailing edge wing); legs orange-yellow.
(Male.) Bill dark grey; dark crescent-markings on breast; back vermiculated grey, rump appears very dark in flight; under-tail black, neighbouring area of under-parts grey.
(Female.) Bill grey with much orange at sides; breast dark brown; more slender than female mallard (14*a*) ....
GADWALL (p. 110)

    b. (Both sexes.) Medium; bill shorter and smaller than that of other surface-feeders, blue-grey with black tip; legs grey-brown.
(Male.) Head chestnut with forehead and crown yellow-buff; broad white patch on fore-wing; speculum green,

white above, black bars forward and aft; under-tail black, contrasts boldly with white under-parts.

(Female.) Head pink-buff spotted brown; forewing grey-brown; speculum dusky, only faintly green, white above, white bars forward (conspicuous) and aft ....
WIGEON (p. 116)

c. (Both sexes.) Medium-large; long slender neck, pointed tail and wings; bill and legs grey.

(Male.) Head chocolate, with white band down side of neck broadening into white breast; forewing and back mouse-grey; speculum not very prominent, green, glossed with bronze-pink, black above, buff bar forward, white bar aft; under-tail black, contrasts boldly with neighbouring yellow patches on under-parts.

(Female.) Head and forewing brown; speculum bronze-brown with only trace of green, white bar aft ....
PINTAIL (p 118)

17. a. (Both sexes.) Bill and legs grey; forewing brown.

(Male.) Head chestnut, with green band extending back from round eye to nape, outlined in buff; breast boldly marked smallish dark spots; speculum green, black below, buff bar forward, faint white bar aft; back vermiculated grey with white streak; under-tail black, contrasts boldly with neighbouring yellow-buff patches on under-parts.

(Female.) Head brown and white, little trace of eyestripe; breast brown and white, back brown; speculum green, black below, white bars forward and aft...TEAL (p. 112)

b. (Both sexes.) Legs grey; back dark brown: under-tail white and brown.

(Male.) Bill black; head rich brown, with fairly broad white band curving from above eye to nape; breast golden-brown, with fine crescent-markings, contrasts with pale grey flanks; forewing blue-grey; speculum green, overhung above by long blue-grey, black and white mantle-feathers, white bars forward and aft.

(Female.) Bill green-grey; head brown and white, with more distinct eyestripe than female teal (a); breast brown; forewing ash-brown; speculum obscure, faint green, no overhanging mantle-feathers, white bars forward and aft
GARGANEY (p. 114)

18. a. Short bodied, squat ducks; legs set back, have to walk with body carried nearly vertically, not horizontally as

surface-feeders; rise from water by pattering (except goldeneye); bills short, 'duck-like' eclipse plumage not marked (except in eiders); wing-action very rapid; feet project beyond tail in flight. . . . DIVING DUCKS; see 19

   b. Long bodied, almost cigar-shaped in flight; on ground body carried more horizontally than *a*, but not so horizontally as surface-feeders; bills slender, tapering (serrated); crest on back of head; long neck held stiffly out in flight . . . . SAW-BILLS; see 27

19. DIVING DUCKS

   a. Small-medium or medium; fresh-water, or partly so; straight rustling flight, often high; under-parts white (except pochard and (summer) tufted females) . . . . . . see 20

   b. Medium or medium-large; almost wholly marine; heavier but rapid flight, nearly always low; under-parts dark
                                 see 24

20. *a.* Small-medium or medium; males with chestnut head. . . .
                                  see 21

   b. Medium; males with black head . . . . see 22

21. *a.* Medium. Sexes unlike. No white on wing.
     (Male.) Bill light blue, black base and tip; head chestnut; breast black; back and flanks vermiculated light grey; under-parts white; rump and under-tail black; legs dull grey.
     (Female.) Bill black, blue a big spot only; whole body dull brown (slightly vermiculated) with whitish about base of bill, cheeks and throat; legs greenish-grey. . . . .
                          POCHARD (p. 122)

   b. Small-medium; sexes much alike. Whole upper body rich chestnut; curved white broad band on wing, sometimes invisible at rest but conspicuous in flight; conspicuous white under-tail; blackish bill and legs; male has white round eye, female brown. . FERRUGINOUS DUCK (p. 124)

22. *a.* (Both sexes.) Bill short; head of triangular outline; back, rump and wings black, with broad white patch extending over most of *inner* half of wing nearly to leading edge; under-parts (and under-tail) white; legs orange.
     (Male.) Bill blackish; head black with green and purple gloss, and round white patch between bill and eye; neck and breast white.

(Female.) Bill blackish, yellow at tip; head chocolate; adults have whitish collar; flanks and breast-bar mottled grey . . . . GOLDENEYE (p. 130)

b. (Both sexes.) Bill normal size, blue-grey; broad white wing-bar extending across almost whole of *trailing* half of wing—quite unlike a; under-tail dark; legs blue-grey. (Male.) Head, breast, rump and under-tail black; belly and flanks white.

(Female.) Generally dark brown . . . . see 23

23. a. (Male.) Head black, with tuft hanging from the back of it; back black.

(Female.) Small amount of white at base of bill; belly white, but brown in summer; under-tail dark brown . . . .
TUFTED DUCK (p. 126)

b. Bill wider and more spatulate than a's.

(Male.) Head black, glossed green, no tuft; back vermiculated pale grey.

(Female.) Broad white band round base of bill, forming white face; belly white, brown at edges and flanks only in summer; under-tail black . . . . SCAUP (p. 128)

Immature female scaups do not have white faces and are *extremely difficult* to tell from immature female tufteds.

24. a. Males pied . . . . · . . . . see 25

b. Males black . . . . see 26

25. a. (Both sexes.) Medium; flight swinging; small, usually whitish, head with steep forehead and short bill; no white on wings; under-parts and flanks white; sharp pointed tail.

(Male.) Mainly dark brown and white; bill pink or orange with black base and tip; central tail feathers about 5 inches long; in winter white on crown, throat, nape, upper breast and sides of back, leaving grey-white face and brown patch on side of neck, brown breast-band and mid-back-line; in summer this white nearly all replaced by rich brown; unique crooning call, 'loudl-oudl-ow'.

(Female) Bill blackish; head mostly white with brown crown and sides of neck; back brown; under-parts white with brown chest-band. Juveniles darker, and grey below
LONG-TAILED DUCK (p. 132)

b. (Both sexes.) Medium-large; flight strong and steady; bulky form; short neck; head large, flat line of forehead continued along beak; tail not pointed.

(Male, normal plumage.) Bill blue-grey and green; head white, with black crown and green nape; breast pinkish; under-parts and flanks black; back white, black rump with white patch on sides; wing black with whole fore-wing white; legs olive-yellow to green; voice 'ah-oo'.

(Female.) Brown barred with black; bill and legs greenish dusky; two obscure light wing-bars...................
COMMON EIDER (p. 134)

26. *a.* (Male in full eclipse.) Medium-large. Blackish; light streak from bill to, and round eye; fore-wing white, patch visible when bird at rest, and in flight occupying *leading* half of inner half of wing; tail not pointed...................
COMMON EIDER (p. 134)

b. (Both sexes.) Medium. No wing-bar; tail pointed.

(Male.) Entirely black; bill black, large knob, and con-spicuous yellow patch; legs blackish; voice 'wor-lee'.

(Female.) Dark brown; bill blackish; side of head pale browny-white; legs brownish ....
COMMON SCOTER (p. 136)

c. (Both sexes.) Medium-large. Conspicuous white wing-patch, occupying *trailing* half of inner half of wing; tail pointed.

(Male.) Black; bill black, smaller knob, most of sides of bill orange-yellow; small white patch behind eye; legs deep red; voice 'whur-er'.

(Female.) Dark brown; bill blackish; two white patches, one in front of, the other behind, and both just below, eye; legs dull red...........VELVET-SCOTER (p. 138)

27. SAW-BILLS

a. (Both sexes.) Small-medium; small short grey bill, grey legs; white belly; high forehead; flight extremely rapid, agile and swinging; rise easily straight from water.

(Male.) White, except for black patch below eye, black centre of crest, black bands on sides and flanks, black centre to back and black wings, on which prominent white patch occupying most of leading half of inner half.

(Female and immature.) Head chestnut, with clear white chin, throat and cheeks, upper-parts grey; wing grey-black with slightly smaller white patch than male's on its inner half................................SMEW (p. 144) *b.* (Both sexes.) Medium-large or large; long red bill and legs, low forehead; white patches on inner half wing; flight fast and straight but heavy; rise by pattering.

(Male.) Bill and legs bright red; head bottle-green; back black; rump and tail grey.

(Female.) Bill and legs dull red; head chestnut, crested; white patch on throat; back and flanks grey......see 28

28. *a.* Large. (Male.) No crest; breast and flanks white and, with under-parts, suffused with more or less salmon-pink; fore-wing grey, behind which inner half of wing almost fully occupied by clear white patch that joins white of sides of back and neck.

(Female.) Crest, hangs down back of head; chestnut of head and neck sharply separated from grey of body; back ash-grey; clear contrasting white throat-patch.........|

GOOSANDER (p. 140)

b. Medium-large. (Male.) Crest; breast chestnut, separated from green head by white collar; flanks vermiculated grey; under-parts white; fore-wing black, behind which broad white patch is crossed by two black bands; this patch occupies most (but not all) of inner half of wing and extends some way on to sides of back, and in front of wing but, though conspicuous, is not so conspicuous as that of goosander.

(Female.) Crest, does not hang down back of head; chestnut of head shades gradually, in neck, into grey of body; back brown-grey; white throat-patch dingy and not clearly contrasting....................................

RED-BREASTED MERGANSER (p. 142)

FIELD CHARACTER KEY TO BRITISH GREBES AND DIVERS

Grebes and divers can be distinguished from most other water-fowl by their gait and posture. In flight they are cigar-shaped (like saw-bills), with their heads and necks held stiffly out, sometimes lying in a lower plane than the line of their backs, giving a hunched appearance. On the water they appear tail-less (like some diving ducks). When landing they strike the water breast-first (unlike any duck), and all except the red-throated diver patter along the surface of the water before taking off.

1. *a.* Small to medium. Necks long and slender, held normally erect when swimming; most have head-plumes in breeding season; most have conspicuous white wing-patches. Nestlings striped......................GREBES; see 2
   b. Medium-large or large. Necks moderately long, stouter than *a*, held normally curved when swimming; no head-plumes in breeding season; no white patches on wing. Nestlings not striped..................DIVERS; see 6

2. GREBES
   a. Medium; relatively long-billed; winter appearance upper-parts brown and under-parts white; two white patches on wing ....see 3
   b. Small medium or small; relatively short billed; winter black and white; one (rear) patch on wing ....see 4
   c. Small; relatively short-billed; winter brown and light....
   see 5

3. *a.* The largest grebe. In winter, bill pink; ear-tufts and crest persist; top of head looks flattened and angular; white line between blackish crown and eye; back dark grey-brown. In summer, bill red; remarkable 'tippet' of chestnut on side of head which hangs over neck as frill..
   GREAT CRESTED GREBE (p. 146)
   b. Bill black with yellow base. No crest; or ear-tufts in winter; in winter top of head rounded; black crown extends down to eye; back darker brown than *a*. In summer front and sides of neck chestnut; cheeks pale grey with white border ....RED-NECKED GREBE (p. 148)

4. *a.* Small-medium. Bill dark; whitish tip. In winter usually indistinguishable from *b* at a distance; but bill is straight and relatively stout, and dark colour of crown does not extend below eye, and white on face and sides of neck almost meets on back of neck. In summer neck and breast chestnut, head and tippet black; and prominent group of buff feathers extends from eye back and up as tufts or horns .... SLAVONIAN GREBE (p. 150)
   b. Small. Bill dark; whitish tip. Bill slender and usually tip-tilted (but not *always* so). In winter black of crown usually extends below eye and well down over ear-coverts; white on cheeks, etc., does not extend towards nape but leaves continuous broad dark line down back of neck. In breeding season forehead much steeper, and crown more peaked

than *a*; neck black; tuft of buff-gold feathers extends back (not up) fan-wise from eye, to form 'ears'; shyer than *a* and tends to swim with neck curved...............
BLACK-NECKED GREBE (p. 152)

5.   More squat than 4; wide stern. White on wing like other grebes but patch not conspicuous. No head ornaments; neck relatively short and thick; bill stouter than 4, black, extreme tip light, yellow-green at base. In winter upperparts medium brown, under-parts whitish-brown, cheeks and sides of neck buff. In breeding-season dark brown with cheeks, throat, and front of neck chestnut........
DABCHICK (p. 154)

6. DIVERS

a. Medium-large. Bill slender, up-tilted, pale grey. In winter upper-parts greyer than those of *b* and speckled with fine white spots; crown and back of neck grey. In breeding-plumage head and sides of neck ash-grey-brown; back dark grey-brown, uniform dull red throat-patch (looks dark). Can 'jump' from water; haunts small lochs......
RED-THROATED DIVER (p. 160)

b. Medium-large or large. Bill thicker, evenly tapered, black. In winter upper-parts dark, or very faintly barred; crown and back of neck grey-brown. In breeding-plumage pattern of black and white on upper-parts. Patter to take off; haunt large lochs.............................see 7

7. *a.* Large. A good deal heavier than *b* and bill very stout and heavy. In winter head slightly darker than back, and in adults back very faintly barred white. In breeding-season head and neck black with purple and green gloss; an incomplete collar and short throat-band formed of vertical white streaks show as light patches; entire upper-parts conspicuously spotted and barred white; under-parts white with black streaks on side of breast.............
GREAT NORTHERN DIVER (p. 156)

b. Medium-large. In winter head slightly lighter than back, and back darker and more uniform than *a*. In breeding-season head and back of neck grey; front of neck black; back and scapulars show marked area of broad white bands, rest of back black; sides of neck and breast have long vertical black and white streaks.................
BLACK-THROATED DIVER (p. 158)

BIRD RECOGNITION

II

BIRDS OF PREY AND
WATER-FOWL

SNOWY OWL *Nyctea scandiaca* (LINNAEUS, 1758)

RECOGNITION. Medium-large. Length, males about 21 in., females about 24 in. Weight about 4½ lbs. White; males almost purely so, with a few brown spots, females white barred with brown boldly on upper-parts, and (less boldly) on under-parts except face, throat, and upper breast, which are white; eyes yellow; bill and claws blackish. Flies over open country boldly by day, sometimes soaring, and kills in air by stooping, on ground by pouncing on birds and mammals of all kinds, and occasionally beetles, spiders, and fish. Ejects pellets. Occasionally shrieks but is mostly silent.

DISTRIBUTION AND MOVEMENTS. Breeds round tundras, coasts and some islands of Polar Basin, from Lapland east through Siberia, Alaska and the Canadian Arctic to Greenland. Recently discovered nesting in Iceland. Numbers depend on, and fluctuate with, the numbers of chief prey—lemmings and voles; extent of movements south in winter, and the numbers that move, is highly variable. After a highly successful season snowy owls appear in unexpected places throughout temperate Europe, Asia, and North America. In Britain are seen nearly every year Shetland, and often in Orkney, North Highlands and Western Isles.

TO READ. V. E. Shelford (1945). *The relation of snowy owl migration to the abundance of the collared lemming.* Auk, vol. 62, pp. 592–96. Dennis Chitty, Helen Chitty, Charles Elton and Mary Nicholson (1937–45). *Canadian Arctic wild life enquiries, 1935–43.* Journal of Animal Ecology, vols. 6, pp. 368–85; 7, pp. 381–94; 8, pp. 247–60; 9, pp. 227–42; 10, pp. 184–203; 11, pp. 270–87; 12, pp. 163–72; 14, pp. 37–45.

SNOWY OWL, male, about 1/7.

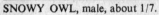

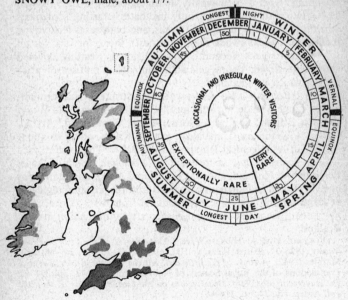

LITTLE OWL   *Athene noctua* (SCOPOLI, 1769)

RECOGNITION. Small; the smallest British owl. Length about 9 in. Weight 5-7 oz. Round and plump; head flat. Upper-parts brown, or grey-brown spotted with white; under-parts buff-white, or grey-white streaked with dark brown. Has a 'fierce' look. Flight by day frequent, sinking like woodpeckers between series of beats of rounded wings. Runs on ground. Hunts mostly at dawn and dusk, eating insects, mammals, earthworms and birds (in that order of volume consumed), also reptiles, amphibians, fish, crustaceans, spiders, centipedes, millipedes and molluscs. Ejects pellets. Haunts park- and farm-land; sometimes tree-less islands. Voice 'kiew kiew' outside breeding-season.

BREEDING. Solitary. Male has pairing call, loud 'hoo hoo'; female shrieks during copulation; and both sexes utter soft 'oo oo'. Female begs food from male with note 'sree sree' like young birds in nest. No apparent sexual display beyond these sounds, but male often flies to nest-hole after mating. Nests in holes in trees, walls and ground; sometimes in old birds' nests, no lining. Eggs 3–5, normally 4, exceptionally 8 or 9, length $1\frac{1}{4}$–$1\frac{1}{2}$ in., matt white. Hen only incubates (starting sometimes when first egg laid) for 4 to $5\frac{1}{2}$ weeks, and both sexes feed young from 4 to 5 weeks (when they leave nest), thenceforward for up to 5 further weeks. Second brood occasional. Nestling covered short white down. Young gets adult plumage in first season after that in which it is hatched.

DISTRIBUTION AND MOVEMENTS. A strict resident through-out its range, wandering only locally. Breeds through Old World west to Britain; south to North Africa, Somaliland, Arabia, Persia, Afghanistan, Himalayas; east to Korea, north to about lat. 55° in Asia, central Russia and the Baltic. The western race *Athene noctua vidalii* is resident in Portugal, Spain, France, Belgium and Holland, and was introduced into England in Kent in *c.* 1874, and in Northants. by Lord Lilford, breeding regularly at large for the first time near Oundle from 1889; since when has spread, see maps. Also established after introduction in New Zealand.

TO READ. Miss A. Hibbert-Ware (1937). *Report of the little owl food inquiry*, 1936–37. British Birds, vol. 31, pp. 162–87, 205–29, 249–64. B. J. Marples (1942). *A study of the little owl*, Athene noctua, *in New Zealand.* Transactions of the Royal Society of New Zealand, vol. 72, pp. 237–52. Fr. Haverschmidt (1946). *Observations on the breeding habits of the little owl.* Ardea, vol. 34, pp. 214–46.

LITTLE OWL, about 3/10.

Black dots: centres on introduction, birds present 1889. Dark grey: breeding range by 1909; medium grey: by 1929; light grey: 1930 and after.

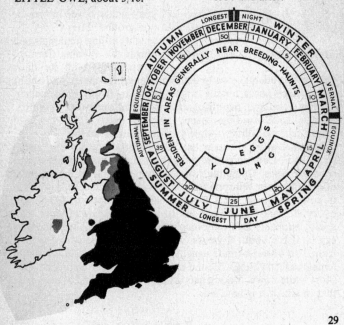

29

LONG-EARED OWL   *Asio otus* (LINNAEUS, 1758)

LONG-EARED OWL, about 2/11.

RECOGNITION. Small–medium. Length 14 in. Weight about 11 oz. Smaller than tawny owl. Ear-tufts prominent when erect, but usually held flat and quite invisible. Iris of eye yellow —distinguishes from tawny owl. Upper-parts mottled grey-buff and brown; under-parts buff, with broad brown longitudinal streaks and rather faint transverse bars. Wings and tail longer than tawny owl's, and wings broader and rounder than short-eared owl's. Looks greyer than short-eared owl. Quite nocturnal; spends day under cover in tree or on ground. Flies silently by night, killing mammals and birds by nipping through their skulls with its claws (primarily rodents, mostly field-voles and field-mice), and eating a few insects; occasionally catches trout and frogs. Ejects pellets. Haunts woodland, mainly coniferous; occasionally open country. Silent outside breeding-season.

BREEDING. Solitary. Male's song is slow moan 'oo—oo—oo', very penetrating. Female has less penetrating, sighing 'soo—shoo—oo'. Courtship zigzag flight among trees, clapping wings, by both sexes. Coughing notes at nest-site. Nests in old nests of other birds or squirrels and sometimes on ground, exceptionally in holes, no lining. Eggs 3–5, normally 5, exceptionally 8, length 1½–1¾ in., matt white, laid sometimes at intervals of more than a day. Probably hen only incubates (starting usually when first egg laid) for about 4 weeks, and both sexes feed young in nest from 3 to 4 weeks (male usually, but not always, brings food to female to feed young). Second brood occasional. Nestling covered short white down. Young gets adult plumage in first season after that in which it is hatched.

DISTRIBUTION. Breeds in the Old World west to Ireland, north to Lapland and Siberia, east to north Japan, south to China, the Himalayas, Afghanistan, Persia, Asia Minor, North Africa, the Canaries and the Azores; in the New World west to the Pacific, north to MacKenzie, Hudson's Bay and southern Quebec, east to Newfoundland, and south to the southern United States. Northern elements migrate in winter to southern part of this range, including Britain, and beyond to north India, south China, south Japan, central Mexico and Gulf States of U.S.

MOVEMENTS. British breeding resident; but a small, not quite regular, passage of birds from northern Europe through Shetland, Orkney and down east coast in autumn, returning in spring. The commonest owl of Ireland, which has no little, tawny or short-eared owls.

TO READ. C. B. Ticehurst (1939). *On the food and feeding-habits of the long-eared owl* (Asio otus otus). Ibis, series 14, vol. 3, pp. 512–20. E. J. Hosking (1941). *Some notes on the long-eared owl*. British Birds, vol. 35, pp. 2–8.

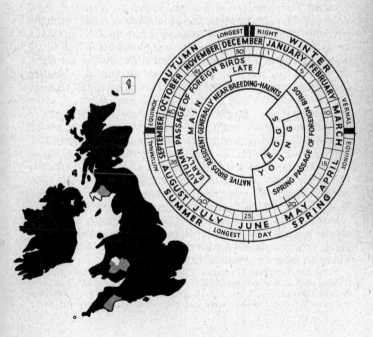

SHORT-EARED OWL

Asio flammeus (PONTOPPIDAN, 1763)

RECOGNITION. Small-medium. Length 15 in. Weight 11-14 oz. Ear-tufts never prominent, and usually held flat and invisible. Lighter than and not so streaked as long-eared owl. Upper-parts marbled (rather than mottled as in long-eared owl) buff and brown; under-parts buff streaked brown—no trace of transverse bars; wings and tail barred, wings markedly long, narrower and less rounded than those of long-eared owl. More diurnal than nocturnal; lives on open ground and hunts silently, often 'quartering' a stretch of moorland mainly for field-voles, also for field-mice, other small mammals, adult and young birds and insects. Ejects pellets. Occasionally cries 'kear' while hunting.

BREEDING. Solitary. Song is reverberating 'boo-boo-boo . . .'' uttered in circling display-flight, in which bird claps wings, flaps and glides, and drops in air after uttering note. Nests on ground in heather, grass or reeds, lined a few stems. Eggs 4–8, normally 6; when field-voles (or in Europe, lemmings) abundant 9–14, length $1\frac{1}{2}$–$1\frac{3}{4}$ in., matt white, laid at intervals of 2 days or more. Hen only incubates, starting to do so before the last egg is laid, for $3\frac{1}{2}$ to 4 weeks, and male brings food for female to feed young in nest for about a fortnight, and near it for another fortnight, after which they can fly. Second brood occasional. Nestling covered short down, buff and white. Young gets adult plumage in first season after that in which it is hatched.

DISTRIBUTION. Breeds in Old and New Worlds north to beyond arctic circle; south to Pyrenees, Mediterranean, central Asia and Manchuria, south-west, central and north-eastern U.S. Not in Ireland or Iberia. Also breeds (other races) in Pacific (Caroline, Hawaiian and Galapagos Is.), Caribbean (Hispaniola and Porto Rico) and western and southern S. America. Elements of main race move south in winter to N. Africa, Arabia, N. India, S.E. China, central America and Gulf of Mexico.

MOVEMENTS. British breeders appear to be mostly resident; a regular passage of northern birds, marked in vole- and lemming-years, very noticeable on each coast route; many birds stay for winter on moors and coastal flats.

TO READ. T. Russell Goddard (1935). *A census of short-eared owls* (Asio f. flammeus) *at Newcastleton, Roxburghshire,* 1934. [*ditto*], 1935. Journal of Animal Ecology, vol. 4, pp. 113–18, 289–90. R. Chislett (1941). *Behaviour and some habits of the short-eared owl.* Naturalist for 1941, pp. 205–14.

SHORT-EARED OWL, about 2/9.

TAWNY OWL *Strix aluco* LINNAEUS, 1758

TAWNY OWL, about 2/11.

RECOGNITION. Small-medium. Length about 15 in. Weight, male 13-17 oz., female 18-23 oz. Brown, sometimes greyish-brown (also very rare grey form). Larger than long-eared owl, and fatter, with head larger in proportion. No ear-tufts. Eye black, not yellow. Upper-parts red-brown and dark-brown, mottled and streaked, with some small very light patches, under-parts buff, with some broad longitudinal streaks of brown; some faint transverse bars can also be seen, usually. Wings broad and rounded. Quite nocturnal, hunts woodland, farm-land and sometimes built-up areas, and kills mostly field-mice, field-voles and rats, also other small mammals, birds (sometimes beating them out of their roosts), fish, amphibians, insects, slugs, earthworms and some vegetable matter. Ejects pellets. Call- and hunting-note 'ke-wick', but song (see later) heard every month of year.

BREEDING. Solitary. Male's song is hunting 'hoo-hoo . . . . oo-hoooooo', very penetrating, answered by female with 'ke-wick'. In display flight male claps wings; on branch sways, puffs out plumage, and raises and stretches wings. Frantic aerial chases with many weird notes, in which rôle of sexes not clear. Nests in holes in buildings, trees, and sometimes ground, and in old nests of birds or squirrels, unlined. Eggs 2–4, normally 4, exceptionally 7, length 1¾–2 in., matt white, laid at intervals of 2 days or more. Hen only incubates (starting when first egg laid) for about 4 weeks, and both sexes feed young for 4 or 5 weeks; male brings most food to female who feeds young, but female catches some food herself. One brood only. Nestling covered short white down. Young gets adult plumage in first season after that in which it is hatched.

DISTRIBUTION AND MOVEMENTS. A strict resident throughout its range, wandering only locally. Breeds through Old World
west to Scotland, England, Wales and Portugal, north to south
Sweden, central Russia, Turkestan and Manchuria, east to Korea
and Formosa, south to north Burma, Himalayas, Baluchistan,
Persia, Asia Minor and North Africa. A dozen subspecies of
which British race, *Strix aluco sylvatica*, is confined to British
Isles (though lumped by some with the birds from France and
Iberia).

TO READ. W. A. Cadman (1934). *An attacking tawny owl*. British Birds,
vol. 28, pp. 130–32. N. Mayaud (1939). *Notes sur le chouette hulotte*. Alauda,
vol. 11, pp. 210–25. Eric J. Hosking and Cyril W. Newberry (1945). *Birds
of the night*. London, Collins, account of all British owls.

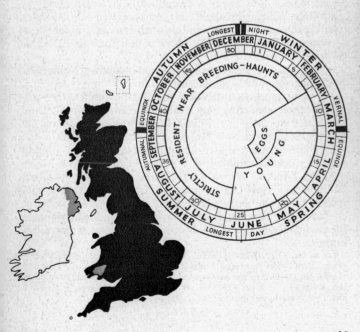

BARN-OWL *Tyto alba* (SCOPOLI, 1769)

RECOGNITION. Small-medium. Length about 14 in. Weight 8-12 oz. Pale as a ghost. Upper-parts orange-golden-buff, mottled with patterns of grey and white; more grey on female than on male. Face and under-parts quite white (dark-breasted form, rare wanderer to Britain, has these buff). Nocturnal and diurnal; often hunting some time before dusk and after dawn, chiefly common shrews and field-voles, commonly field-mice, bank-voles, rats and house-mice, and sometimes other mammals, birds, fish, frogs, and insects. Kills mammals and birds by nipping through their skulls with claws, usually of left foot. Ejects pellets. Haunts farmland and usually hunts in the open. Voice a sinister shriek; possibly hoots, but if so exceptionally rarely.

BREEDING. Solitary. Song includes shriek, but in courtship other sounds. Male claps wings in display-flight; presents food to female; in mutual courtship display much twittering, bill-snapping, cheek-rubbing, snoring and swaying. Nests mostly in buildings, also in tree-holes, rock-crevices and old nests, lined old pellets. Eggs 4–7, normally 5, exceptionally 11, length $1\frac{1}{2}$–$1\frac{3}{4}$ in., matt white, laid at intervals of 2 days or more. Hen only incubates (starting sometimes but not as a rule when first egg laid) for about $4\frac{1}{2}$ weeks, and both sexes feed young in nest for 9 to 12 weeks. Quite often a second brood. Nestling mostly covered short white down, replaced at *c.* 2 weeks by long light buff down. Young gets adult plumage in first season after that in which it is hatched.

DISTRIBUTION AND MOVEMENTS. A strict resident throughout its range, wandering only locally. Breeding pairs in England and Wales estimated at *c.* 12,000 (1932). Breeds over almost the entire world (except New Zealand and Antarctica) south of the line central-northern United States – Azores – Britain – South Sweden – Poland – south-central Russia – Crimea – Asia Minor – Arabia – India – Burma – Indo-China – south-east Asia (not Philippines) – New Guinea – Society Islands. Thirty-four sub-species of which the white-breasted race, *Tyto alba alba*, is confined to Britain, south-west Europe and the Mediterranean; the dark-breasted race, *Tyto alba guttata*, is found in the rest of Europe.

TO READ. G. B. Blaker (1933). *The barn-owl in England. Results of the census.* Bird Notes and News, vol. 15, pp. 169–72, 207–11. C. B. Ticehurst (1935). *On the food of the barn-owl and its bearing on barn-owl population.* Ibis, series 13, vol. 5, pp. 329–35. C. B. Moffat (1940). *The notes of the barn-owl.* Irish Naturalists' Journal, vol. 7, pp. 289–92.

BARN-OWL, about 1/4.

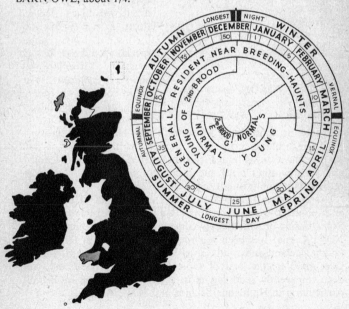

GYR-FALCON, ICELAND FALCON, GREENLAND FALCON

Falco rusticolus LINNAEUS, 1758

ICELAND FALCON, about 1/8
(see also p. 165)

RECOGNITION. Medium-large. Length up to 2 ft.; female longer than male. Weight about 3½ lbs. Larger and slower than peregrine. Tail relatively long. Colour relatively uniform. No well-marked 'moustache'. Wings broader and blunter than peregrine's; wing-beats slower. Gyr-falcon, *F. r. rusticolus*, has upper-parts grey with slight moustache (but much lighter than peregrine's), under-parts whitish streaked and barred with black; Iceland falcon, *F. r. islandus*, usually (but not always) lighter, especially on head, has no moustache; Greenland falcon, *F. r. candicans*, overlaps in colour with Iceland falcon (but not gyr-falcon) but is usually much lighter, and often is almost pure white, with only black flecks on upper parts and black wing-tips. Stoops swiftly at grouse and ptarmigan, also lemmings (not Iceland), duck, waders, seabirds and various other birds and rodents. Ejects pellets. Voice rare outside breeding-grounds, chattering 'kiek'.

DISTRIBUTION AND MOVEMENTS. A falcon of the tundra and sub-arctic wastes, breeding in a chain of subspecies round the Polar Basin; of which the gyr-falcon (northern Scandinavia and N.W. Russia) has been recorded twice in Britain, the Iceland falcon (Iceland and south Greenland) is a rare vagrant, and the Greenland falcon (rest of Greenland, Baffin Island, etc.) has been apparently recorded most often of the three in Britain, particularly in Highlands, Islands and N.W. Ireland.

TO READ. E. Lewis (1938). *In search of the gyr-falcon. An account of a trip to north-west Iceland.* London, Constable. G. P. Dementiev and N. N. Gortchakovskaya (1945). *On the biology of the Norwegian gyr-falcon.* Ibis, vol. 87, pp. 559–65.

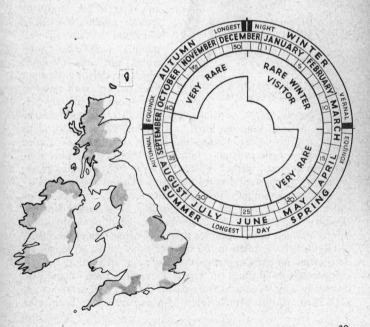

PEREGRINE FALCON

Falco peregrinus TUNSTALL, 1771

DUCK-HAWK in North America.

PEREGRINE FALCON, female, about 1/6 (see also p. 164)

RECOGNITION. Medium. Length about 18 in.; female (30–48 oz.) larger than male (20–28 oz.). The largest falcon breeding in Britain. Tail relatively short, tapering. Upper-parts dark blue-grey, under-parts buff-white barred with black. Black crown, sides of head and 'moustache'. Long pointed wings. Bill bluish yellow at base. Legs and feet yellow, thick and powerful. Flight direct, powerful and fast, a succession of quick beats and long glides. Stoops at speeds which have been estimated as up to 180 m.p.h., with near-closed wings, on birds in flight which it kills by slashing back or neck with claws in full stoop. Usual prey pigeons, grouse, ducks or rooks, but kills also very many other species of land- and sea-birds and waders. Occasionally takes birds, rodents, shrews, frogs, and beetles on ground, and even fish. Ejects pellets. Highly individual, though two birds may sometimes hunt together. Voice rare away from breeding-place, where many chattering notes based on syllables 'kek' and 'e-e'.

BREEDING. Solitary. Probably pairs for life. Unpaired males take territories, in which are discovered by unpaired females. Display consists of excited aerobatics, including looping the loop, in which both falcon (female) and tiercel (male) take part. Nests in Britain, often in old nests of other birds, on ledges on sea- or inland cliffs, sometimes on buildings; in Europe, but not apparently in Britain, in trees. Unlined scrape. Eggs 2–6, normally 3 or 4, laid at intervals of 2 or 3 days, oval, length 2 to 2¼ in., whitish with variable red-brown markings. Both sexes incubate for 4 to 5 weeks, usually starting with second egg. Male at first passes food to female brooding young; both bring food to young in nest after about 2 weeks. Young (usually only 2 survive) tended in nest 5 or 6 weeks, sometimes still fed after departure. Nestling has rather complex succession of downs; at about a fortnight, when may be left alone on ledge, has long down, grey above, cream-white below. Some young cannot be distinguished from adults in first breeding-season after that in which they are hatched; none can be distinguished in second.

DISTRIBUTION. Widely distributed throughout the world, though absent from Central America, tropical South America, New Zealand and some Pacific islands. European race is *F. p. peregrinus*. In Britain resident and passage-migrant.

MOVEMENTS. Birds from northern Europe move south in winter, but others apparently disperse to good feeding-grounds, not necessarily south. In Britain passage in autumn and spring of Scandinavian (and probably Scottish) birds; peregrines hunting in England in winter may be dispersed residents.

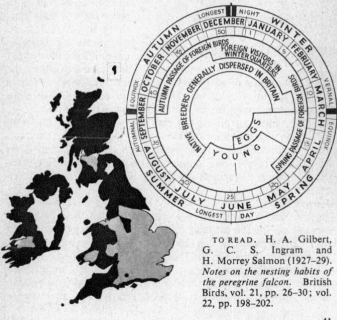

TO READ. H. A. Gilbert, G. C. S. Ingram and H. Morrey Salmon (1927–29). *Notes on the nesting habits of the peregrine falcon*. British Birds, vol. 21, pp. 26–30; vol. 22, pp. 198–202.

HOBBY *Falco subbuteo* LINNAEUS, 1758

HOBBY, about 2/9 (see also p. 164)

RECOGNITION. Small-medium. Length about a foot, female (8–12 oz.) larger than male (5–7 oz.). The most agile falcon breeding in Britain. Tail comparatively short. Upper-parts dark blue-grey, under-parts white streaked with black. Crown and sides of head dark brown, 'moustache' black, conspicuous. Adults have red thighs and undertail. Bill blue. Skin round nostrils and eyes yellow, legs and feet yellow, very slender compared with peregrine's. Wings long, shape of swift's (especially those of tiercel—male). Flight most rapid and manoeuvrable; the finest interceptor of all British birds. Sometimes soars in circles to great heights. Stoops with wonderful grace, often slashes but mostly seizes prey in air, and lives primarily on swallows, martins, larks and pipits, but can take swifts in air, and also eats many other species of birds up to medium size, bats and large insects. Ejects pellets. Not always individual, may hunt in small parties. Voice commoner away from breeding-place than peregrine's, variants on 'kiew', 'kwee', and 'kirik', often chattering and noisy.

BREEDING. Solitary. Displays complex; in air pair circle together and loop. Ceremonial presentation of food to female by male on tree, in attitude showing red feathers of flank, after which male excitedly flies about. Ceremonial passing of food from male to female in air. Nests in trees in old nests of other species (mostly crows). Eggs 2–4, normally 3, laid at intervals of 2 or 3 days, length 1½ to 1¾ in., whitish, yellowish or pinkish finely spotted with brown. Falcon mostly, but also tiercel, incubates for about 4 weeks, starting with second egg. Male at first passes food to female brooding young; both bring food later. Young tended in nest 4 to 5 weeks and fed after departure. Nestling has pale down at first; later grey on back. Most young cannot be distinguished from adults in the first breeding-season after that in which they are hatched; none can be distinguished in the second.

DISTRIBUTION. Breeds through the whole of Europe and Asia, north entirely or almost to the forest-line, south to north-west Africa, Asia Minor, Persia, the Himalayas and China; migrates south to winter in Africa, India and other countries south of breeding-range. To south-east Britain a summer visitor.

MOVEMENTS. Some evidence for coastal passage to and from British breeding-haunts; birds passing in East Anglia and Kent in autumn may be from Scandinavia.

TO READ. Desmond Nethersole-Thompson (1931). *The field-habits and nesting of the hobby.* British Birds, vol. 25, pp. 142–50. G. Schuyl, L. Tinbergen and N. Tinbergen (1936). *Ethologische Beobachtungen am Baumfalken* (Falco s. subbuteo L.). Journal für Ornithologie, vol. 84, pp. 387–433.

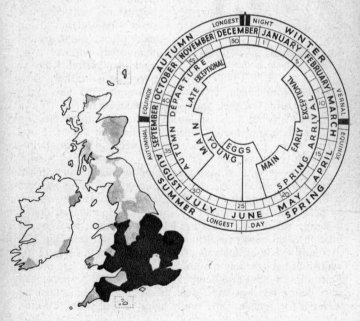

MERLIN *Falco columbarius* LINNAEUS, 1758

PIGEON-HAWK in North America.

MERLIN, male, about 1/4
(see also p. 165)

RECOGNITION. Small. Length 11 or 12 in.; female (7–8 oz.) larger than male (5–6 oz.). The smallest falcon breeding in Britain. Tail longer than hobby's with black band. Upperparts dark blue-grey, underparts buff or red-buff streaked with dark brown. Crown dark blue-grey. Sides of head not uniformly dark. No 'moustache'. Bill bluish, yellow at base. Skin round nostrils yellow, round eye bluish. Legs and feet yellow. Wings less narrow and pointed than hobby's. Flight hurried and swift, alternate quick wing-beats and glides, more often close to ground than other falcons; more agile than kestrel. Kills, by overtaking rather than stooping from height, chiefly meadow-pipits, but also many species of birds and their young up to, and even beyond, its own size, e.g. lapwing and rock-dove; quite often takes prey on ground, including shrews, rodents, reptiles and insects. Ejects pellets. Voice variants of 'kik', 'kek', 'kweep', often chattering, mainly at breeding-place.

BREEDING. Solitary. Males are found, or joined, in territories by females; show ownership by soaring. Courtship includes ceremonial feeding of female by male, and probably aerobatics by both sexes. Nests usually on ground on moorland or dunes, a scrape, often among heather or marram-grass; occasionally on cliff-ledges, rarely (in Britain) in old nests in trees. Eggs 3–6, normally 4, laid at intervals of 2 or 3 days, length $1\frac{1}{2}$ to $1\frac{1}{4}$ in., whitish or light densely spotted with purple or chocolate-brown. Falcon mostly, but also tiercel, incubates for 4 or 5 weeks; may start before last egg laid. Male passes food to, or sometimes leaves it for, female; only rarely helps to feed young directly.

Young tended in nest 3½ to 4 weeks. Downs of nestling much as other falcons, yellow-white at first, greyish after. Some young cannot be distinguished from adults in the first breeding-season after that in which they are hatched; none can be distinguished in the second.

DISTRIBUTION. A bird of the moorland, plains and open woodland of the northern Old and New Worlds. Breeds in Iceland, Faeroe, N.W. Britain, Europe north and east of the Baltic, northern Asia and northern North America, north in many places beyond the arctic circle and the forest-line (e.g. breeds in Novaya Zemlya). Migrates south in winter, some as far as north and south shores of Mediterranean, Asia Minor, northern India, China, Mexico and the Caribbean shores.

MOVEMENTS. Most British breeders disperse shortish distances (in Britain) in winter; but marked passage (especially autumn) along east coast, and lesser passage along west of birds which breed in Iceland and Scandinavia.

TO READ. William Rowan (1921–22). *Observations on the breeding-habits of the merlin.* British Birds, vol. 15, pp. 122–29, 194–202, 222–31, 246–53.

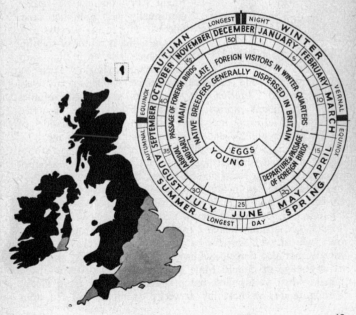

45

KESTREL *Falco tinnunculus* LINNAEUS, 1758

KESTREL, male, about 1/5
(see also p. 164)

RECOGNITION. Small-medium. Length about 14 in. Female (6–9 oz.) longer than male (5–8 oz.). The longest-tailed falcon breeding in Britain; tail as long as sparrow-hawk's. Tail of male grey with broad black band, white tip beyond; of female barred. Upper-parts rufous (or chestnut, adult male) spotted or barred with black; under-parts buff streaked with black. Head of adult male grey, of others rufous. No 'moustache'. Wings pointed like merlin's—distinguishes from sparrow-hawk. Bill bluish, pale at base. Skin round nostrils and eye yellow. Legs and feet yellow. Flight very distinctive; hovers continually; less agile than other falcons. Hovering, mostly over open ground, is means of sighting prey which is taken in flight only exceptionally; mostly kills, by clutching on ground (or perch) field-mice (*Apodemus*) and voles (*Microtus* and *Clethrionomys*), also bats, small birds, reptiles and frogs, insects, worms, and snails. Ejects pellets. Usually, though not always, individual hunter. Voice succession of variants on 'kee', 'kik' and 'kek', mostly at breeding-place.

BREEDING. Solitary. Display consists of pursuit of and stooping at, and courtship-feeding of, female by male. May attempt to copulate in air. Nests on cliff-ledges, in trees and occasionally on buildings, often in old crow's nests and nests of other large birds. Site sought by male and female, with special ceremonies. Flattens old nests; on ledge unlined scrape. Eggs 3–7, normally 4 or 5, laid at intervals of 2 to 4 days, length 1½ in. or a little over, whitish with variable patches and spots of brown. Falcon mostly, but also tiercel, incubates for about 4 weeks, may start at any stage of clutch. Male leaves food for, or passes it to female when young first hatch, later may feed them direct. Young tended in nest for 4 weeks or more, and fed after

46

departure. Down of nestling at first white, later greyish. Males attain adult plumage in third season after that in which they are hatched, females in second. Females may breed in the first summer after that in which they are hatched, in non-adult plumage.

DISTRIBUTION. A small-rodent-eater of open or semi-open land in the Old World. Breeding-range is west to Britain, Canaries, Madeira and Cape Verde Is., south to South Africa, Ceylon and Burma, east to Japan, north to Central Siberia, north Russia in Europe and Scandinavia. Some elements migrate south in winter.

MOVEMENTS. Most British breeders disperse shortish distances (in Britain) in winter, a few may migrate as far as Spain; but marked spring and autumn passage along east coast of Britain, and lesser passage along west of birds that breed in northern Europe and N. Scotland.

TO READ. L. Tinbergen (1940). *Beobachtungen über die Arbeitsteilung des Turmfalken* (Falco tinnunculus L.)' *während der Fortpflanzungszeit*. Ardea, vol. 29, pp. 63–98. J. C. S. Ellis (1946). *Notes on the food of the kestrel*. British Birds, vol. 39, pp. 113–15.

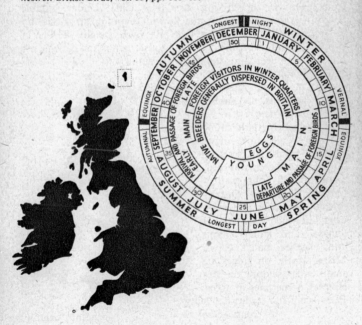

GOLDEN EAGLE *Aquila chrysaëtus* (LINNAEUS, 1758)

RECOGNITION. Immense. Length 2½ to nearly 3 feet; female (9½–13 lbs.) larger than male (7½–11 lbs.) Can be confused with buzzard in flight, as outline similar, until observer realizes scale and power of bird. Head of eagle projects further, and even at a distance huge beak shows. Plumage of adult golden eagle dark tawny-brown. Young golden eagle has white tail with broad, black band at end. Head of white-tailed eagle is light, tail shorter and more wedge-shaped than golden eagle's. Golden eagle has tarsi ('shins') feathered to base of toes (unlike w-t e). Bill not so deep as w-t e's, black, grey at base, and skin round nostrils and toes yellow. Wing-spread 6–7 ft., sometimes more. Flight stately and magnificent, usually slow beats and long glides; deceptively fast; has been seen to fly 3½ miles at 120 m.p.h., rising 1,000 ft. net. May stoop at flying prey, in close-wing dive, snatching birds up (not striking them down), but mostly 'flies down' birds and mammals on ground. Two or three may co-operate in driving hares from cover, or in separating deer-calves from hinds or (rarely) lambs from ewes, or in driving deer over cliffs. Under suitable conditions an eagle can lift and fly with a trap or an animal up to but probably not more than its own weight. Feeds in Scotland mainly on blue hares; on grouse, lambs and ptarmigan; also on red deer and roe-deer calves, and rabbits; occasionally on other mammals, several kinds of medium to very large birds, and salmon and pike. Ejects pellets nearly 4 in. long. Individual, though hunts in family groups in autumn. Voice rare, mewing yelp or whistle, and alarm-bark. Young cry like cats in nest.

BREEDING. Solitary. Probably pairs for life. Display mostly aerobatics and evolutions in which male pursues female, and female loops and touches male's claws. Nests mostly on ledges or small cliffs (seldom on precipices), sometimes in trees. Pairs use a few traditional sites,

Distribution in nineteenth century.

continued p. 51

W 266

GOLDEN EAGLE, about 1/10 (see also p. 166)

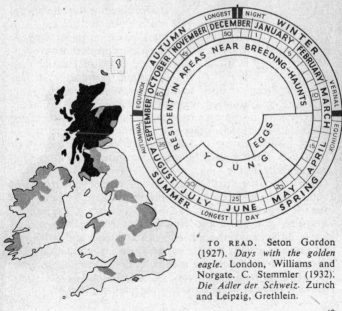

TO READ. Seton Gordon (1927). *Days with the golden eagle*. London, Williams and Norgate. C. Stemmler (1932). *Die Adler der Schweiz*. Zurich and Leipzig, Grethlein.

ROUGH-LEGGED BUZZARD

Buteo lagopus (PONTOPPIDAN, 1763)

Hawk in N. America.

ROUGH-LEGGED BUZZARD,
about 1/8 (see also p. 166)

RECOGNITION. Medium. Length up to 2 ft., female (35–41 oz.) larger than male (26–35 oz.) Majestic soaring flight, and general shape, may cause confusion with eagles. Distinguished in flight from most common buzzards by lightness of under-parts and under-wing (though common buzzards very variable and some almost as light). Good point is black band on under-tail, near tip, apparently broader and more prominent on rough-legged buzzard, because on near-white background, whereas band (and bars) on tail of common buzzard always on darkish background. Also dark patch on under-wing always more prominent on rough-legged buzzard. Heavier than common buzzard, and legs feathered. Prospects open country in slow tacks, often taking long 'legs' and hovering (more than common buzzard) when prey suspected; eats mostly rodents, in breeding-range lemmings, in Britain rabbits, also other small mammals, birds to size of pintail, game-birds (up to hen capercaillie), a few small birds and insects. Ejects pellets. Mewing voice stated to be lower than common buzzard's.

DISTRIBUTION AND MOVEMENTS. A bird of sub-arctic open country and the arctic tundra, breeding where lemmings are found (except in some parts of the high arctic), and south to the forest-line of the Old and New Worlds. Nearest breeders to Britain in Norway; in north and east Scotland, and north and east England a fairly regular winter visitor. Migration of north European breeders does not usually reach Mediterranean.

TO READ. H. N. Southern (1946). *Studies of some species rarely photographed. I. The rough-legged buzzard.* British Birds, vol. 39, p. 48.

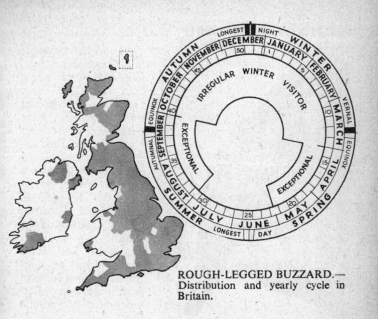

ROUGH-LEGGED BUZZARD.—Distribution and yearly cycle in Britain.

GOLDEN EAGLE—*continued*

to which both birds bring much material in year of use, often ferns and grass. Eggs 1–3, normally 2, length $2\frac{3}{4}$ to $3\frac{1}{2}$ in., whitish, very variably spotted brown and grey, laid at intervals of 3 or 4 days. Female, relieved very rarely, if at all, by male, incubates for six or seven weeks, starting with first egg. Young (never more than two survive) fed by both parents (chiefly male) on nest 11 weeks or more. Nestlings pass through usual three downs, all white. Young gets adult plumage in fourth or fifth season after that in which it is hatched.

DISTRIBUTION AND MOVEMENTS. A bird of open and mountain country, breeding in Old and New Worlds south to north-west Africa, Syria, Persia, Himalayas, N. China, Japan and Mexico, north to about forest-line. In Britain breeding-range, reduced to Highlands and Islands, shows recent signs of slight extension and recovery. Stock highly resident, though young disperse and wander, occasionally into England and Ireland.

51

COMMON BUZZARD   *Buteo buteo* (LINNAEUS, 1758)

COMMON BUZZARD, about 1/7
(see also p. 166)

RECOGNITION. Medium. Length about 21 in., female (25–42 oz.) larger than male (22–31 oz.). Liable to be confused with eagles, and rarer rough-legged buzzard. Upper-parts brown; under-parts light with variable amount of brown bars and streaks; lightest form not so light as rough-legged buzzards, and dark mark on underwing not so pronounced. Under-tail has black band and bars on darkish background (distinct from rough-legged buzzard where background light). Not as large or heavy as rough-legged buzzard, and in flight circles more and hovers less. Legs and feet yellow, not feathered. Drops in silent glide and clutches live prey on ground; also eats carrion. Chief food in Britain rabbits; other rodents (especially voles), moles and carrion also important; and eats other mammals, and any birds it can get (up to woodpigeon and pheasant size, though not certain these taken alive), reptiles and amphibians, insects, molluscs and bilberries. Ejects pellets. Usually individual, but small flocks not rare. Voice a mewing 'meeoo, peeoo', other notes at breeding-place.

BREEDING. Solitary. Various soaring, gliding and diving display-flights. Large nests built by birds, certainly by female, not proved if also by male; male may, as part of display, pass decoration-material to female. Nests of sticks usually much embellished (throughout occupation) with small leafy branches. Eggs 1–6, normally 2 or 3, laid at intervals of 3 days, length 2 to 2½ in., bluish-white with variable pattern of dark brown spots and stains. Both sexes incubate for 4 to 5½ weeks, starting with first egg. In first fortnight after hatching male brings food to female; afterwards both feed young direct. Young in nest 6 or 7 weeks and fed after departure. Nestlings first down white, later grey. Young attain adult plumage in first or second season after that in which they are hatched.

DISTRIBUTION AND MOVEMENTS. A bird of forest, wood-. land and forest-edge of Europe, breeding in Norway to about the arctic circle, but not further north; in south to Mediterranean, with outposts on the Atlantic islands (Azores, Madeira, Canaries, Cape Verdes); in east to Balkans, Russian border and Baltic states; replaced beyond by the steppe-buzzard *Buteo vulpinus* (opinion is divided as to whether it should be regarded as of same species). In Britain a resident, spreading in the north and west (not Ireland), apparently non-migratory: autumn and winter birds that wander in eastern England may be of Continental origin.

TO READ. Arthur Brook (1920). *The buzzard at home*. London, Witherby. V. Wendland (1933). *Vermehrung, allgemeine Brutbiologie und Ernährung des Mäusebussards* (Buteo b. buteo). Beiträge zur Fortpflanzungsbiologie der Vögel, vol. 9, pp. 157–67. G. H. Ruck (1944). *Buzzards*. Journal of the Society for the Preservation of the Fauna of the Empire, new series, part 49, pp. 23–27.

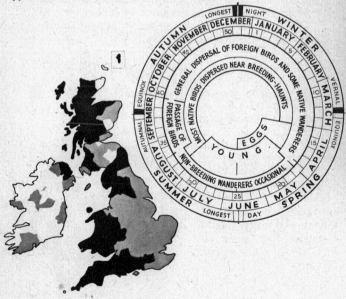

MARSH-HARRIER *Circus aeruginosus* (LINNAEUS, 1758)

RECOGNITION. Medium-large. Length about 21 in. Female (22–26 oz.) longer than male (17–22 oz.) A typical harrier with long tail and legs. Largest British harrier. Wings, though long, more rounded than those of other harriers. Females, males and juveniles are dark brown, with some light on head: but male has wide grey band across wings and grey or buff tail (rest of upperparts brown, *not* grey) which contrasts with black ends to wings; good recognition-character. Flies close to ground, with flaps and glides, and pounces to clutch prey; eats mainly frogs and young of game-birds, also grass-snakes, rodents, eggs or young of many other birds, some small adult birds, fish and carrion. Ejects pellets. Individual hunter. Voice rare away from breeding-grounds, where various coos, mews and whistles.

BREEDING. Solitary. Male has display-flight with aerobatics, brings food-gifts to female. Nest in marsh of reeds and stems lined grass, built by hen. Eggs 3–7, usually 4 or 5, laid at intervals of 2 to 4 days, length $1\frac{3}{4}$ to $2\frac{1}{4}$ in., blue-white. Female mostly, occasionally male, incubates 5 or 6 weeks, usually starting on first egg. Young fed at nest 5 or 6 weeks by female, which takes food in air-pass from male. Down of nestling at first white or grey-white, pink above. Females attain adult plumage in second, males in third season after that in which they are hatched.

DISTRIBUTION AND MOVEMENTS. Marshes and fens of Europe and C. Asia, breeding west to E. Anglia; north to S. Sweden, Finland and C. Russia; east to Yenesei and Mongolia; south to Turkestan and shores of Mediterranean. Winters south into tropical Africa and Asia. British breeders much reduced; under 10 pairs in Norfolk and Suffolk, but bred N. Wales 1945. British breeders, or wanderers from Continent, have been seen in spring and autumn in many English counties, and some in Ireland, Wales and Scotland.

Distribution in nineteenth century.

W 271

MARSH-HARRIER, male, about 1/7 (for immature male see p. 163)

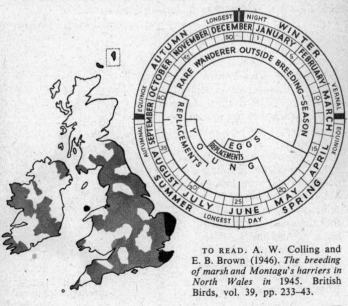

TO READ. A. W. Colling and E. B. Brown (1946). *The breeding of marsh and Montagu's harriers in North Wales in 1945.* British Birds, vol. 39, pp. 233–43.

MONTAGU'S HARRIER

Circus pygargus (LINNAEUS, 1758)

RECOGNITION. Medium. Length up to 18 in. Female (9–15 oz.) larger than male (8–11 oz.). Smaller than marsh-harrier, wings narrower, less heavy in flight. Females have barred tails—those of msh. have not; but females and juvenile males of Montagu's hard to distinguish from those of hen-harrier. Mgu. females slighter, have a narrower and 'dirtier' white patch on upper-part tail, and narrower wings; their juveniles unstreaked buff underneath whereas those of h.-h. markedly streaked. Males both species have grey upper-parts and black wing-ends; the Mgu. male has dark bar across wing which shows on under-wing, grey rump and reddish-looking flanks; the h.-h. male has no such wing-bar, conspicuous white rump, no red on flanks. Chestnut streaks also on male Mgu. under-parts; those of male h.-h. unstreaked grey. Hunts, as msh., mainly reptiles and amphibia (eats adders) and in breeding-season young birds and eggs; also rodents, adult small birds, insects and worms. Ejects pellets. Voice mainly at breeding-place, whickering and cooing. Female screams to male.

BREEDING. Sometimes social. Display-flights with aerobatics. Nests on marsh or moor of reeds and grasses, mostly built by hen. Eggs 3–6, usually 4 or 5, laid at intervals of 2 or 3 days, length $1\frac{1}{2}$ to $1\frac{3}{4}$ in., turquoise-white stained brown. Female incubates 4 to 5 weeks, starting on first egg. Young fed at nest for 4 to 5 weeks by female, which takes food in air or on ground from male; Downs of nestling light buff. Females attain adult plumage in second, males in third season after that in which they are hatched.

DISTRIBUTION AND MOVEMENTS. Fens and open marshy moorlands, much the same breeding-distribution as msh., though not nesting quite so far N. or S. Migrates for winter further than msh., some reaching S.W. Asia and S. Africa. Number nesting Eng. and Wales shows signs recent recovery. Almost unknown Britain November to March.

Distribution in nineteenth century.

MONTAGU'S HARRIER, male, about 1/6 (for female see p. 163)

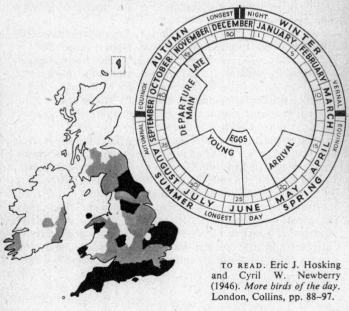

TO READ. Eric J. Hosking
and Cyril W. Newberry
(1946). *More birds of the day*.
London, Collins, pp. 88–97.

HEN-HARRIER   *Circus cyaneus* (LINNAEUS, 1766)

MARSH-HAWK in North America.

RECOGNITION. Medium. Length 18 in. or more. Female (14–19 oz.) larger than male (10–14 oz.). Male's upper-parts are grey, paler than those of Montagu's, upper part of tail pure white; under-parts, throat and breast delicate grey, rest white (no chestnut), with a few 'ghost-bars' (not streaks) of grey; wings grey with black ends. Female, like female Mgu's, has upper-parts dark brown and under-parts light brown streaked with dark brown —streaks on h.—h. female being rather more pronounced; upper-part of tail has purer white patch than has Mgu's. Juvenile has streaked under-parts, which juvenile Mgu's has not. Rather more active and positive hunter than other harriers, but quarters ground in same style, pursuing or dropping mainly on rabbits, voles, mice and pipits; also on other rodents, water-shrews, reptiles and frogs; and eggs, young and adults of birds up to size of grouse (particularly waders and passerines), fish and beetles. Ejects pellets. Individual hunter. Voice rare away from breeding-place, whence whickers, coos and squeals recorded.

BREEDING. Solitary. Male's display-flight includes somersaults and dives, and chasings of female. Nest on moorland in scrape lined by hen with grasses and stems. Eggs 3–6, usually 4 or 5, laid at intervals of 2 to 4 days, length $1\frac{1}{2}$ to 2 in., blue- or turquoise-white, sometimes spotted brown. Female alone incubates for 4 to 5 weeks, starting on second egg. Young fly after 5 or 6 weeks in which they are probably fed by female alone, to which food passed by male; may be fed a further 3 weeks by both parents direct. Down of nestling at first white, later buff. Young attains adult plumage in second season after that in which it is hatched.

DISTRIBUTION AND MOVEMENTS. A bird of open moorland and bog of Old and New Worlds, breeding north in Europe, Asia and North America as far as forest-line, to Portugal, N. Spain, France, Sicily, Balkans (not Greece), Caucasus, Turkestan, N.E. Siberia, Lower California, Texas, R. Mississippi and Virginia. In Britain only regular breeder now in Outer Hebrides and Orkney, but shows recent signs of recovering lost status in N. Highlands, and breeds occasionally Border country, Wales and England. Migrates in winter as far as N. Africa, S. Asia and shores of Caribbean; British breeders may not leave islands, and birds possibly from Scandinavia visit Britain on passage and in winter.

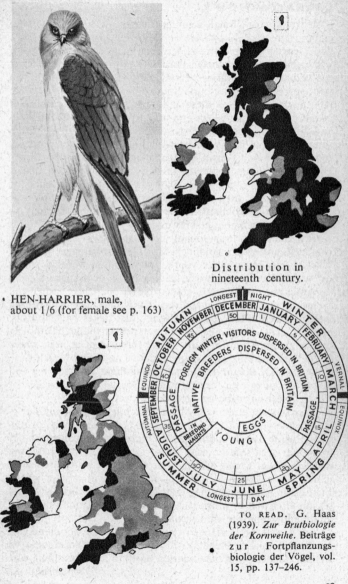

Distribution in
nineteenth century.

HEN-HARRIER, male,
about 1/6 (for female see p. 163)

TO READ. G. Haas
(1939). *Zur Brutbiologie
der Kornweihe.* Beiträge
z u r Fortpflanzungs-
biologie der Vögel, vol.
15, pp. 137–246.

SPARROW-HAWK *Accipiter nisus* (LINNAEUS, 1758)

RECOGNITION. Small-medium. Length male (4–6 oz.) about a foot, female (7–10 oz.) about 15 in. Upper-parts, male dark grey, female grey-brown; under-parts male russet barred with white, female whitish finely barred with brown. Female has white eye-stripe. Plumage varies a good deal, and juveniles have brown upper-parts and under-parts spotted and flecked rather than truly barred. But even these under-parts distinct from those of kestrel which are streaked, and broad rounded wings, long legs and distinctive method of hunting also make identification simple. Goshawk is very much larger. Flies in fast glides (probably reaching 60 m.p.h.) down woodland rides, round hedge-corners and farm-buildings, and even through apparently dense undergrowth, usually capturing small birds in air or off ground by surprise, though often by superior speed and manoeuvrability. Takes prey to feeding-platforms outside breeding season. One sparrow-hawk possibly kills as many as a thousand small birds a year, chiefly starling (young), house-sparrow, hedge-sparrow, chaffinch, greenfinch, goldfinch, linnet, yellowhammer, great tit, blue tit, meadow-pipit, sky-lark, robin, willow-warbler, white-throat, blackbird, song-thrush, fieldfare, stock-dove, wood-pigeon, domestic pigeon, lapwing, golden plover, partridge (adult and young), pheasant (young) and very many other species; has been seen to attack adult cock pheasants; also takes bats, weasels, moles, rodents, frogs and insects. Ejects pellets. Individual, though may sometimes hunt in pairs. Voice rare except at nest, where harsh loud 'kekking', and many plaintive notes and whistles.

BREEDING. Solitary. Mutual display-flight with soaring and mock stooping over nesting-wood. Special diving-display of female. Nest normally on high tree in wood, often on old nest of other species, built mainly by female. Eggs 3–7, usually 4 or 5, laid at intervals of 1 to 3 days, length 1½ to 1¾ in, blue- or turquoise-white usually spotted with dark brown. Female incubates (male *has* been seen on nest) for 4½ to 6 weeks usually starting on second egg. Young fly after 3 or 4 weeks in which are fed by female alone, to which food passed by male at nest or in air. First down is white, nestling later greyish. Young breeds in first season after that in which it is hatched but sometimes does not attain adult plumage until second.

DISTRIBUTION AND MOVEMENTS. A bird of woodland and wooded farmland, breeding through the Old World west to Ireland, Madeira and the Canaries, north to the forest-limit, east
continued p. 63

SPARROW-HAWK, female, about 2/9 (see also p. 165)

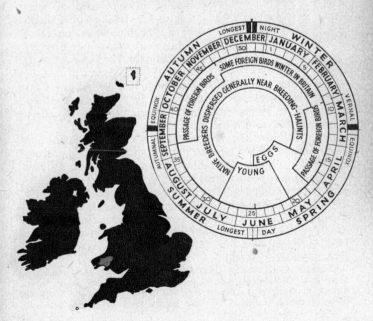

GOSHAWK *Accipiter gentilis* (LINNAEUS, 1758)

GOSHAWK, female, about 1/8

RECOGNITION. Medium-large. Female, 22–23 in. (37–44 oz.) longer than male, 19–20 in. (23–26 oz.). Plumage closely resembles female sparrow-hawk's, but very much larger—longer than peregrine, with which can be confused until tail is spread. Hunts, jinking with great speed and agility, usually through woodland, and kills by clutching very many kinds of mammals and birds up to size of hares and capercaillie but perhaps most often thrushes. Ejects pellets. Alarm-note chattering 'gek-gek'.

BREEDING. Solitary. Display-flights. Nest built by female usually in high woodland tree. Eggs 2–5, normally 3 or 4, length 2¼ to 2½ in., blue-white, sometimes lightly marked brown. Hen mostly incubates for 5 or 5½ weeks. Male brings food to female at nest for 3 weeks after young hatch, then both feed young direct for further 3 or 4 weeks, after which young fly. Nestling's downs are greyish-white. Young attains adult plumage in second season after that in which it is hatched, but may breed in first.

DISTRIBUTION AND MOVEMENTS. A bird of the forest and forest-edge of Old and New Worlds, breeding north to the forest-line, south to the Mediterranean, Balkans, Black Sea, Caspian Sea, Himalayas, South China, Japan, N. Mexico and western and northern United States. Western European subspecies *A. g. gentilis* and chief American subspecies *A. g. atricapillus* have both been recorded in Britain, latter 6 times only. Former is rare wanderer, mostly to E. England, but pairs attempted to breed Lincolnshire 1864, laid eggs Yorkshire 1893, attempted to breed England 1948, succeeded 1949-50.

TO READ. Horst Siewert (1933). *Die Brutbiologie des Hühnerhabichts.* Journal für Ornithologie, vol. 81, pp. 44–94, and various papers by P. Ruthke, C. Demandt, the Baron Geyr von Schweppenburg and D. König (1929–38) in the Beiträge zur Fortpflanzungsbiologie der Vögel, vols. 5, 9,

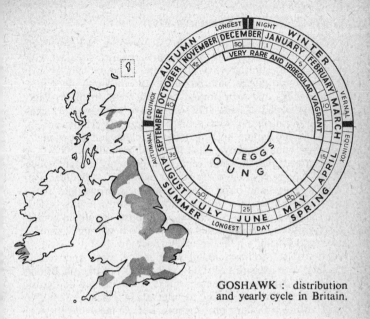

GOSHAWK : distribution and yearly cycle in Britain.

13 and 14. R. Meinertzhagen (1950). *The goshawk in Great Britain.* Bulletin of the British Ornithologists' Club, vol. 70, pp. 46-49.

SPARROW-HAWK—*continued*

to Kamchatka and Japan, south to China, Burma, the Himalayas, Persia, Asia Minor, the south shore of the Mediterranean and Morocco. Ten subspecies recognised, of which those in Asia appear to be migratory, those in Europe and North Africa mostly resident. British native birds probably resident, but distinct passage of Continental birds along east coast of England, autumn and spring; some stay for winter.

TO READ. Many papers by J. H. Owen (1915–36) in British Birds, vols. between 8 and 30. O. Schnurre (1932). *Zur Ernährungsbiologie des Sperbers* (Accipiter nisus *L.*). Journal für Ornithologie, vol. 80, pp. 247–57. J. Sokolowski (1933). *Observations sur la biologie de l'Épervier* (Accipiter nisus *L.*). Ochrona Przyody Warszawa, vol. 13, pp. 103–23. Hubert E. Pounds (1936). *Notes on the flight of the sparrow-hawk.* British Birds, vol. 30, pp. 183–89. L. Tinbergen (1946). *De sperwer als roofvijand van zangvogels.* Ardea, vol. 34, pp. 1–213.

KITE *Milvus milvus* (LINNAEUS, 1758)

RECOGNITION. Large. Length 2 ft. or over. Weight about 35 oz. Upper-parts brown; under-parts reddish, streaked with dark. Head of adult grey, or grey-white, of young light brown. Can only be confused with buzzards, and then only until long narrow wings and very forked tail are seen. In flight wings markedly 'angled' at joint, and, seen from below, have black ends beyond conspicuous white patches. Flight powerful, slanting, banking, gliding and soaring, often circling and occasionally hovering. Food list shows most taken on ground—kite's skill is in detection rather than interception; eats mainly carrion, young rabbits, young poultry, other young mammals and birds; also adult mammals and birds to size of squirrels, grouse and duck; and frogs, reptiles, fish, insects and earthworms. Ejects pellets. Often hunts or scavenges in flocks, and roosts socially in winter. Voice whistle and high-pitched mew, very distinct from buzzard's, also various trilling notes in breeding season.

BREEDING. Solitary. Display-flights by male and female together, and massive nest built by both in tall tree, in Britain in hanging oakwood, with many sticks, much rubbish and grass. Eggs 2 to 4, normally 3, laid at intervals of 3 days, length 2 to 2½ in., white with faint brown spots. Female incubates for 4 or 5 weeks, with some relief from male, starting on first egg. Young fly after 6 to 8 weeks, in first two of which are fed by female alone, to which male brings food, afterwards by both parents. First down of nestling is white, later creamy buff. It is not known how soon the young attains adult plumage.

DISTRIBUTION AND MOVEMENTS. A bird of wooded foothills, parkland and farmland in Europe (extending a little way into Asia), west to Wales, Portugal and Canaries, north to S. Sweden (has bred Norway) and Baltic, east to Baltic States, R. Dneiper, Caucasus and N. Persia, south to Palestine, Mediterranean, N.W. Africa and Cape Verde Islands. N. European birds migrate to Mediterranean but not across Sahara. In Britain a remnant resident population in Central Wales; about six pairs attempt to breed each year with varying success, the situation having been about the same for fifty years. Birds, mostly young, disperse (from Wales ?) and wander occasionally into various English and Scottish counties, and bred in Devon in 1913 and probably in 1947, and in Cornwall in 1920 (not on map).

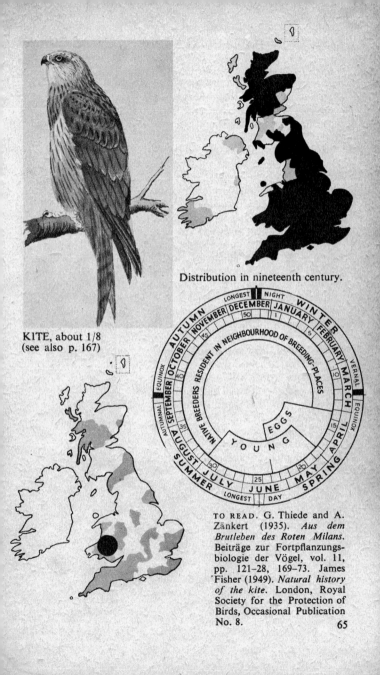

KITE, about 1/8
(see also p. 167)

Distribution in nineteenth century.

NATIVE BREEDERS RESIDENT IN NEIGHBOURHOOD OF BREEDING-PLACES

YOUNG

EGGS

AUTUMN — SEPTEMBER OCTOBER NOVEMBER DECEMBER JANUARY FEBRUARY — WINTER
LONGEST NIGHT
AUTUMNAL EQUINOX
VERNAL EQUINOX
AUGUST JULY JUNE MAY APRIL MARCH
SUMMER — SPRING
LONGEST DAY

50 | 1 | 5 | 10 | 15 | 20 | 25 | 30 | 35 | 40 | 45

TO READ. G. Thiede and A. Zänkert (1935). *Aus dem Brutleben des Roten Milans.* Beiträge zur Fortpflanzungs-biologie der Vögel, vol. 11, pp. 121–28, 169–73. James Fisher (1949). *Natural history of the kite.* London, Royal Society for the Protection of Birds, Occasional Publication No. 8.

WHITE-TAILED EAGLE

Haliaeetus albicilla (LINNAEUS, 1758)

RECOGNITION. Immense. Length up to 3 ft., female (11–14 lbs.) larger than male (*c.* 8 lbs.). Could only be confused with golden eagle. Adults have brown and yellow-white heads and white tails; immature birds dark brown heads and tails, but both have broader (and very slightly shorter) wings and characteristic short wedge-shaped tail, besides deeper and more powerful beak and lower part of tarsi (shins) unfeathered. More clumsy than golden eagle. Hunts by flying heavily over surface of land and water, dropping on prey (may go under for fish). Eats mainly fish, carrion, mammals to size roe, ducks to size eider, puffins, capercaillie, grouse, ptarmigan, adult heron and other birds. Ejects pellets up to 4 in. long. Pairs, and larger groups young birds may hunt and roost together. Voice high chatter, and low cackle.

BREEDING. In Britain usually nested on sea-cliffs, sometimes inland bluffs and islets in lochs. Nest of sticks and weeds, usually lined grass. Eggs 1–3, normally 2, length $2\frac{3}{4}$ to $3\frac{1}{4}$ in., white. Female mostly, seldom male, incubates for 5 to 7 weeks, beginning with first egg. Young fly after about 10 weeks, during which are fed by female alone, for which male brings food; may be fed by both parents for further 4 to 6 weeks. First down of nestling buff, later grey. Young may attain adult plumage in fourth season after that in which they are hatched, but may not breed until sixth.

DISTRIBUTION AND MOVEMENTS. Now breeds W. Greenland, Iceland (*c.* 10 pairs 1949); N. and E. Europe, and Asia, n. to Lapland, Novaya Zemlya and Arctic river-mouths of Siberia; e. to Kamchatka, s. to Mongolia, Turkestan, Persia, Asia Minor and N.E. Mediterranean, w. now to Balkans, Czechoslovakia, N. Germany, Norway, formerly Sardinia, Corsica (perhaps still), Denmark (Jutland), Britain and Faeroe. Last bred Britain (North Roe, Shetland) 1908. Now occasional wanderer, (often young birds) mostly to e. coast England.

Distribution in nineteenth century.

W 280

WHITE-TAILED EAGLE, about 1/11 (see also p. 167)

Note : all breeding-
records before 1908.

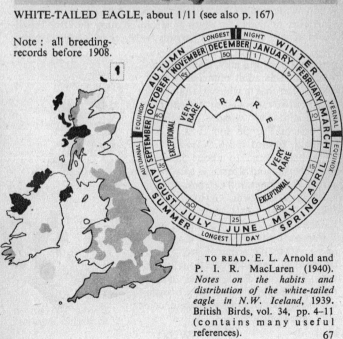

TO READ. E. L. Arnold and
P. I. R. MacLaren (1940).
*Notes on the habits and
distribution of the white-tailed
eagle in N.W. Iceland, 1939.*
British Birds, vol. 34, pp. 4–11
(contains many useful
references).

HONEY-BUZZARD *Pernis apivorus* (LINNAEUS, 1758).

RECOGNITION. Medium-large. Length 21 in. or more. Weight 25–28 oz. General colour variable; upper-parts brown; under-parts from brown to flecked white; head sometimes brown, usually grey, sometimes (young) buff-white on crown. Best recognition characters, and distinction from other buzzards, are: tail longer than buzzard's, with distinctive pattern of broadish (not narrow) dark bands, of which two (sometimes three) on forward half of tail, and one (broadest) near end of after half; wings longer and narrower; head projects further; runs easily on ground. Hunts like buzzard for ground-game, but mainly lives on social insects, digging up their communities with its claws and beak; eats larvae, pupae, adults, combs and honey of wasps, bees, ants; also many insects, small rodents, eggs and young of birds, reptiles, amphibia, molluscs and worms. Ejects pellets. Hunts individually, though sometimes moves in flocks. Voice characteristic squeaky whistle, other notes at breeding-place.

BREEDING. Both sexes decorate old nest of other species. Eggs 1–3, normally 2, laid at intervals of 3 to 5 days, length $1\frac{3}{4}$ to $2\frac{1}{4}$ in., yellow-white richly marked with brown. Both incubate, beginning with first egg, for $4\frac{1}{2}$ to $5\frac{1}{2}$ weeks. Young fly after 5 to $6\frac{1}{2}$ weeks, during which at first fed only by hen to which cock brings food, later by both. First down of nestling cream and grey, later whitish. Young attains adult plumage in first season after that in which it is hatched.

DISTRIBUTION AND MOVEMENTS. Woodland and wooded farmland throughout Europe and Asia, w. to Portugal, France and S. Norway; n. to Lapland, and to about 58° lat. across Russia and Siberia; e. to Japan, Philippines and Celebes; s. to Java, Sumatra, Ceylon, India, Persia, Asia Minor, Balkans, mid-Italy, N. Spain. European birds migrate to c. and s. Africa for winter. Used to breed in England (occasionally Scotland), but has probably nested under ten times in last forty years. Seen occasionally spring and autumn passage e. coast, very rare elsewhere.

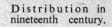

Distribution in nineteenth century.

HONEY-BUZZARD, about 1/7 (see also p. 167)

Note: breeding highly
irregular in black areas.

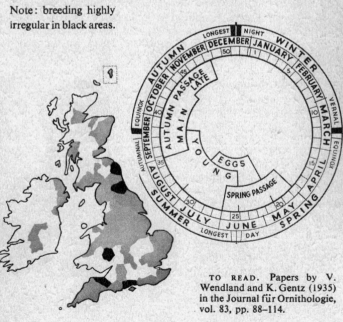

TO READ. Papers by V.
Wendland and K. Gentz (1935)
in the Journal für Ornithologie,
vol. 83, pp. 88–114.

OSPREY *Pandion haliaetus* (LINNAEUS, 1758)

RECOGNITION. Medium-large. Length 21 in. to 2 ft., female larger than male. Weight *c.* 3¼ lbs. Upper-parts brown, flecked with white; head and under-parts (including under-wing) white except for brown breast-band and brown markings on edges and end of under-wing, and brown streak from behind eye widening to back of neck. Legs and feet thick, powerful and greenish. Wings and tail narrow; wings long (4½ to 6 ft. spread) and leading edge angled (not straight as eagles and buzzards). Quarters water-surface, hovers and drops feet-first with near-closed wings from about 50 ft. on to or into water, catching fish of many kinds in claws; spiny scales on inside of toes help hold fish. Often goes right under. Also eats carrion, small rodents, wounded adult birds, young water-birds, frogs and crustaceans. Can carry a fish of its own weight. Ejects pellets. Usually individual, though sometimes flocks on migration. Voice a chipping whistle, a clucking, whickering alarm-note, and others.

BREEDING. Individual in Britain, sometimes social elsewhere. Nested in Britain mostly on rocky islets in lochs, sometimes in pines. Sites traditional and nests cumulative, built by both birds out of every probable, and some improbable materials, lined grass. Eggs 2–4, normally 3, laid at intervals of 2 days, length 2 to 2½ in., white richly marked chocolate. Hen mostly, but also cock, incubates, beginning first or second egg, 5 weeks. Young fly after 7½ to 10 weeks, during which fed only by hen, for which cock brings food to nest. Nestling probably at first cream-buff, but quickly develops pattern of buff head, brown upper-parts, throat and breast, with light dorsal streak and under-parts. Young appear to attain adult plumage in first year after that in which they are hatched.

DISTRIBUTION AND MOVEMENTS. A bird of fresh-water lakes, large rivers and calm coasts of North America, Europe, *continued* p. 73

Distribution in nineteenth century.

W 284

OSPREY, about 1/7 (see also p. 167)

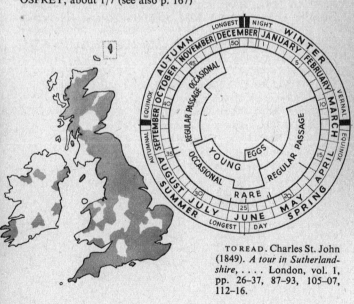

TO READ. Charles St. John (1849). *A tour in Sutherland-shire*, ... London, vol. 1, pp. 26–37, 87–93, 105–07, 112–16.

WHITE STORK   *Ciconia ciconia* (LINNAEUS, 1758)

RECOGNITION. Immense. Length about 40 in., of which body 20 in. Weight males $5\frac{1}{2}$ to $9\frac{1}{2}$ lbs., females 5 to 9 lbs. Most of wing and part of mantle black, rest white. Long red legs. Long red bill, straight and sharply tapered. Flies majestically with neck and legs stretched out. Compare crane, vol. 1, p. 122. Walks and wades in search of food which is mainly frogs; also other amphibia, reptiles, and fish; and insectivores, rodents, young and eggs of birds, insects (particularly locusts), crustaceans, molluscs and worms. Ejects pellets. Often feeds in flocks. Voice billclattering; various other noises particularly at breeding-place.

DISTRIBUTION AND MOVEMENTS. Open cultivated land and marshes in Europe and Asia, breeding in four groups : *C. c. ciconia*, (*a*) n. to S. Sweden and S.E. Baltic; e. to Dneiper Valley, Caucasus and Persia; s. to Iraq, Syria, Asia Minor, Bulgaria, Greece, Yugoslavia, Austria, Switzerland ; w. to Alsace, Germany, Holland and Denmark; *C. c. ciconia*, (*b*) C. and S.W. Spain, S. Portugal and N. W. Africa ; *C. c. asiatica*, Turkestan and neighbourhood; *C. c. boyciana*, Manchuria, Amur River, Korea and S. Japan. Almost complete census in Europe, mostly 1934, gave Switzerland 10, France 155, Holland 273, Denmark 859, S. Sweden, 12, Germany 30,730, Danzig and Poland 8,503, Memel 1,682, Latvia 8,525, Czechoslovakia 2,413, Austria 118, Spain 664 occupied nests. In 1935–36 30,556 in French N. Africa. Subspecies *ciconia* migrates to Arabia, and Africa south of the Sahara (has nested in Cape Province). Nested in Edinburgh in 15th century but otherwise known as a wanderer to Britain, mostly to S.E. England in spring.

TO READ. Horst Siewert (1932). *Störche*. Berlin, D. Reinier. Fr. Haverschmidt (1949). *The life of the white stork*. Leiden, Brill.

WHITE STORK, about 1/0

OSPREY—*continued*

Asia and Australasia, breeding in Old World west to Canaries, Portugal, Spain, Balearic Is., Corsica, Germany and Norway, formerly Scotland; north approximately to the forest-line, east to Kamchatka, Japan, the Philippines, New Guinea, Bismarck and Solomon Is., and New Caledonia (not New Zealand); south to Tasmania, Australia, Java, South China, Himalayas, Arabia, Red Sea, Mediterranean and N.W. Africa (absent as breeder from, though winter-visitor to, Borneo, Sumatra, Malaya, Burma and India); in New World from Pacific to Atlantic, north approximately to forest-line, south to Mexico and the Bahamas. Does not now breed Britain, Denmark, Holland, Belgium, France or Switzerland. European breeders migrate to tropical Africa, Asiatic birds to India and the East Indies, North American birds to south-central South America. In Britain bred widely on islands in suitable lochs in Scotland, from which exterminated largely by collectors in 19th century; last certain breeding-record 1908 (Loch Arkaig, W. Inverness-shire). Now a small but regular number pass, mainly through England, in autumn and spring; most likely to be seen on broads or coastal marshes of Norfolk.

SPOONBILL *Platalea leucorodia* LINNAEUS, 1758

SPOONBILL, about 1/97

RECOGNITION. Large. Length up to 3 ft. of which half is body. Weight about 3¾ lbs. White. Black legs and bill. Bill long and spoon-shaped. Adults have yellow on upper breast and crown of head in breeding season, and crest feathers on head. Young have black wing-tips. Flies like heron, but with neck stretched out. Feeds by sweeping bottom of shallows with bill; eats fish, amphibians and their tadpoles and eggs, insects, crustaceans, molluscs, worms and some plant-stuff. Social as a rule. Rarely grunts; claps bill at breeding-place.

DISTRIBUTION AND MOVEMENTS. A bird of fen, estuary and sea-marsh of the Old World. In Western Europe breeds only in S. Spain and Holland, lately in Denmark, formerly in Britain. More continuous breeding-distribution in suitable fens from Austria through Balkans across Asia to Japan, north to Black Sea and Azov S., Caspian S., Aral S., L. Balkash, L. Baikal and R. Amur; S. to Formosa, China, India, Persian Gulf and Somaliland; W. to White Nile, Egypt, Syria and Adriatic. Last bred in England *c.* 200, in Wales *c.* 350 years ago. European birds pass on migration to Central Africa, and (probably from Holland) regularly visit East Anglia, and often visit some counties of the s. coast of England, in spring, summer and autumn. Rare elsewhere.

TO READ. Bentley Beetham (1910). *The home-life of the spoonbill, the stork, and some herons*, London, Witherby. H. A. Bernatzik (1929). *Ein Vogelparadies an der Donau. Bilder aus Rumänien, Tierwelt, Volksleben.* Berlin, Wasmuth. Fr. Haverschmidt (1935). *Beobachtungen in der Löfflerkolonie im Zwanenwater.* Beiträge zur Fortpflanzungsbiologie der Vögel, vol. 11, pp. 1–3.

GLOSSY IBIS *Plegadis falcinellus* (LINNAEUS, 1766)

RECOGNITION. Medium. Length 22–24 in., of which body 12 in. Weight about 26 oz. Looks black; actually brownish-purple: legs and bill dark; bill down-curved like curlew's. Some white on head and neck in winter. Neck and legs outstretched in flight, wings rounded. Alternate flaps and glides, faster than heron. Feeds like large wader, probing for mud- and water-invertebrates, including insects, molluscs, crustaceans and worms (especially earthworms and leeches); and eats frogs, newts and fish. Sociable as a rule. Voice rare, a croak 'raa', 'graa'.

DISTRIBUTION AND MOVEMENTS. A bird of swamps, slow rivers, and estuaries of the temperate-tropical world, with a somewhat discontinuous breeding-distribution. The subspecies *P. f. falcinellus* breeds in Senegambia, Morocco, S. Spain*, S. France (Camargue)*, N. Italy (Piedmont), Austria (Neusiedler-see), Hungary (Lake Balaton, etc.), Yugo-Slavia (Obedska Bara, R. Vardar near Skoplje, R. Crna Reka near Monastir and L. Ochrida on Albanian border), Rumania, Bulgaria, Russia (Volga and Caucasia), Asia Minor, Syria (Antioch), Egypt and Iraq*, Persia, Russia (Transcaspia, Kirghiz Steppes and Turkestan), Afghanistan, India, Ceylon, Burma ; also in Madagascar. The subspecies *P. f. peregrinus* breeds from the Philippines, Celebes and Java S.E. through the East Indies to Australia. In America a form apparently identical with *P. f. falcinellus* breeds along the coast of the Gulf of Mexico and in Florida, Cuba and Hispaniola, but a white-faced glossy ibis which should probably be regarded as of the same species (*P. f. guarauna*) has a much wider (but apparently not overlapping) distribution in western and southern U.S., and Mexico; and from Brazil (south of the Amazon) and Peru, south to central Argentine and Chile.

European birds migrate in winter as far as South Africa. In Britain an irregular visitor to S. and E. England and S. Ireland, rare elsewhere; most autumn, rare winter and spring.

TO READ. O. E. Baynard (1913). *Home life of the glossy ibis* (Plegadis autumnalis *Linn.*). Wilson Bulletin, Iowa, vol. 25, pp. 103–17. R. F. Bailey (1934). *New nesting records of glossy ibis.* Emu, Melbourne, vol. 33, pp. 279–91.

* Status doubtful.

GLOSSY IBIS, about 1/6

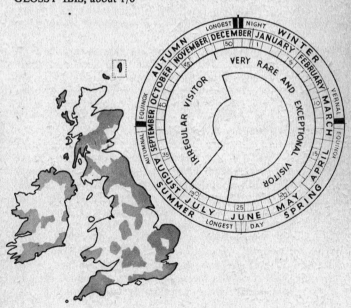

HERON *Ardea cinerea* LINNAEUS, 1758

RECOGNITION. Very large. Length about 3 ft., body about half. Weight 3¼–4½ lbs. Upper-parts, wings and tail grey; ends of wings dark. Head white, with black band (not young) from eye to crest at back of head. Under-parts mostly light grey. Bill yellow (rarely goes red in breeding-season). Legs brown. Ponderous steady flight with head resting back. Feeds by walking slowly, or waiting, in shallow water or on land, to catch by darting strike of bill, with which larger prey impaled. Eats mainly fish, of practically all available species; and reptiles, amphibians (especially frogs), their tadpoles and spawn, rodents (especially water-voles) and other small mammals, adult birds to size of wood-pigeon, young of all available kinds of water-bird, insects of many kinds, crustaceans, molluscs and worms. Ejects pellets of very variable size, some over 3 in. long (mostly contain mammal fur; fishbones are digested.) Usually individual when hunting but may flock occasionally when prey abundant. Voice 'kronk', but at breeding-place many extraordinary sounds and bill-clattering.

BREEDING. Social. Display at heronry, some soaring and circling flights but most ceremonies on nest, including wing-waving, crest-erecting, stretching, snapping. English heronries in trees, bu some Scottish ones on cliffs. Nests traditional and material cumulative; male brings sticks, reeds, and grass to female. Eggs 2–6, normally 4, laid at intervals of 2–4 days, length 2¼ to 2½ in., faintly turquoise. Male and female share incubation for 3½ to 5 weeks, usually starting on first egg, and both feed young in nest for 7 or 8 weeks. Second brood has been observed. Nestling grey-white, very long down on head. Young attains adult plumage in second season after that in which it is hatched, but probably does not breed until third.

DISTRIBUTION. A bird of the waterside of a great variety of country in the Old World, breeding north approximately to the forest-line of Europe and Asia; east to E. Siberia, Japan, Formosa and Hainan; south to Burma, India, Persia, Iraq, Egypt, Crete, Balkans, mid-Italy, Sardinia, N.W. Africa and Canaries (with outpost subspecies in Aldabra, Madagascar and Comoro Is.); west to Spain, France, England, Ireland, Hebrides, Scotland, Orkney and Norway. Appears also to breed occasionally, or locally, in S. and E. Africa, to which some northern Continental (but not British) breeders migrate. In England and Wales breeding population was measured in 1928 at *c.* 4,000 nests in *c.* 300 heronries and remained so (approx.) until 1939. In 1940

HERON, about 1/10

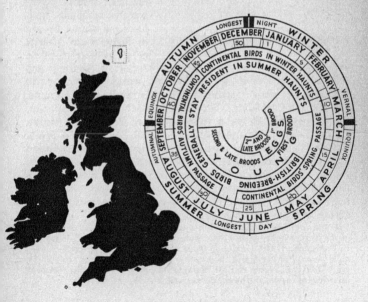

NIGHT-HERON *Nycticorax nycticorax* (LINNAEUS, 1758)

BLACK-CROWNED NIGHT-HERON in North America.

NIGHT-HERON, about 1/6

RECOGNITION. Medium-large. Length *c.* 2 ft., body about half. Weight 26-33 oz. Adult has crown of head and upperparts mostly black, wings and tail grey, under-parts white; legs yellow. Young has dark brown upperparts boldly spotted near-white; under-parts grey with brown streaks; legs greenish. Nocturnal; flies mostly at dusk, head tucked back, feeds at night on freshwater fish of all kinds; also on rodents, amphibians, reptiles, insects, crustaceans, arachnids, molluscs and worms. Croaks in flight, many strange noises at breeding-place.

DISTRIBUTION AND MOVEMENTS. Social. Swamps and marshy waters of temperate-tropical world, breeding n. to Holland, Germany, Czechoslovakia, Austria, Balkans, Ukraine, Don Basin, Caspian S., Turkestan and Mongolia; e. to Japan, Philippines and Celebes; s. to Indian Ocean, Persia, Asia Minor, Egypt, Sicily, Tunis and Morocco; w. to S. Portugal and Spain, France (Camargue and near Lyon on Rhône, and Lac de Grand Lieu near Nantes, Loire) and ? Belgium; in c. and s. Africa: in Hawaii: in America n. to approx. lat. 50° N., w. of Great Lakes (just in Canada), Ottawa and St. Lawrence Rivers, s. to Tierra del Fuego and Falkland Is. Wanderer to Britain, most frequent spring and autumn in E. and S. England.

TO READ. G. K. Noble, M. Wurm and A. Schmidt (1938). *Social behaviour of the black-crowned night heron.* Auk, vol. 55, pp. 7–40. R. P. Allen and F. P. Mangels (1940). *Studies in the nesting behaviour of the black-crowned night heron.* Proceedings of the Linnean Society of New York, vol. 50–51, pp. 1–28. G. K. Noble and M. Wurm (1942). *Further analysis of the social behaviour of the black-crowned heron.* Auk, vol. 59, pp. 205–24.

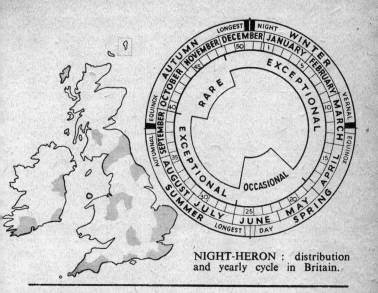

NIGHT-HERON : distribution and yearly cycle in Britain.

HERON—*continued*

(cold winter) began to fall; by 1942 probably under 3,000; rose again to *c.* 4,000 1945 and 1946; fell sharply to not much over 2,000 1947 (very cold winter), no sign of recovery 1948, but *c.* 3,000 nests 1949, nearer 4,000 1950, number Scotland and Ireland not determined as some heronries small and scattered.

MOVEMENTS. Adult English herons seldom move much more than 10 to 20 miles from their heronries. Adults in Scotland, and young everywhere, disperse in winter to greater distances (some north to Shetland) but probably do not truly migrate. Birds breeding from Scandinavia to France are regular passengers and winter-visitors along E.–S. and W. coasts, and strengthen the inland population, especially of England and Ireland.

TO READ. E. M. Nicholson (1929), *Report on the 'British Birds' census of heronries*, 1928, British Birds, vol. 22, pp. 270–323, 334–72; supplements (1930–31), vols. 23 and 25, and annual indices of population to date in vols. 28 (1935) onwards, by Nicholson and (since 1939) by W. B. Alexander. J. Verwey (1930). *Die Paarungsbiologie des Fischreihers.* Zoologische Jahrbücher (für allgemeine Zoologie), Jena, vol. 48, pp. 1–120. J. P. Strijbos (1935). *De blauwe Reiger.* Amsterdam, Veen. N. F. Ticehurst (1939). *The migratory status of the heron in Great Britain.* British Birds, vol. 32, pp. 242–46. Alice Hibbert-Ware (1940). *An investigation of the pellets of the common heron (Ardea cinerea cinerea).* Ibis, series 14, vol. 4, pp. 433–50.

BITTERN   *Botaurus stellaris* (LINNAEUS, 1758)

RECOGNITION. Large. Length about 2 ft. 6 in., of which body slightly less than half. Weight 2¼ to 2¾ lbs. Sexes alike. Crown black, crest tipped buff, upper-parts buff-brown heavily mottled black. Under-parts lighter buff; from chin pale band down over breast ending in bib of long feathers darkly streaked. Dark streaks on rest of buff under-parts become reddish at sides. Bill green-yellow; legs and feet green. Flies usually low, and rather like brown ghost at dusk; neck retracted. At rest may also retract neck to create dumpy compact appearance, or may stretch neck and beak up vertically; both positions may be concealing, latter simulating reeds. Can also assume fear-inspiring attitude by crouching and expanding bib and crest. Walks or runs like other herons. Feeds in heron fashion mainly on fish (particularly eels—has powder-patches on breast producing down with which brushes off eel-slime); also on rodents, shrews, adult birds to size of water-rail, amphibians, reptiles, insects, crustaceans, arachnids, and molluscs. Individual. Voice extraordinary penetrating 'b'wump', often dawn and dusk; other notes on breeding-grounds.

BREEDING. Solitary, though apparent social displays in air at start of season. No other form of courtship so far observed. Nests in reed-beds, built by female, of reeds, lined grass, etc. Eggs 3–7, usually 4, laid at intervals of 2 or 3 days, length 2 to 2¼ in., greenish-brown. Female alone incubates, starting with first egg, for 3½ to 5 weeks (i.e. 3½ for each egg); and alone feeds young, which fly after 8 weeks, though they may wander from nest after just over a fortnight. Nestling red-brown on upper-parts, throat white, under-parts buff. Young attain adult plumage in first season after that in which they are hatched.

DISTRIBUTION AND MOVEMENTS. A bird of reed-beds in the temperate Old World, South Africa and Australasia. *B. s. stellaris* breeds north to S. Sweden, Finland, in Russia the R. Dvina to Archangel, and the head-basins of the Volga, Khirghiz Steppes, S. Siberia, Manchuria and R. Amur; east to Japan; south to N. China, Mongolia, Manchuria, Turkestan, Afghanistan, Baluchistan, Persia, Iraq, Palestine, Mediterranean, Tunisia, Algeria, Morocco; west to Portugal, Spain, France, Britain and Denmark. *B. s. capensis* breeds in S. Africa from Bechuanaland (L. Ngami) to Natal and Cape. *B. poiciloptilus* of Australia, Tasmania and New Zealand should probably be regarded as a further subspecies of *B. stellaris*. Some European birds move for winter to tropical Africa. In Britain a fairly

continued p. 85

BITTERN, about 1/6

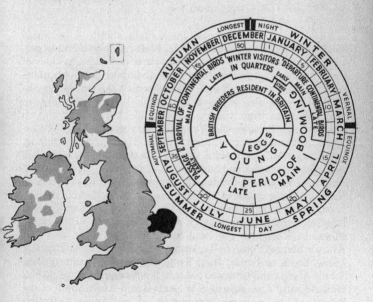

LITTLE BITTERN *Ixobrychus minutus* (LINNAEUS, 1766)

LITTLE BITTERN, male, about 1/4

RECOGNITION. Small-medium. Length about 14 in., body about half this. Weight about 5 oz. Male has crown and·upper-parts black with green gloss; under-parts buff, dark at sides of upper breast. Female has crown black and upper-parts chocolate, and under-parts streaked buff. On both male's and female's upper-wing is a large, almost round light patch (lighter on male): this is conspicuous when the male flies, and clear, though not so contrasting, on the female. Young are very streaked. Bill yellow-green, legs and feet green. Flies with head back and legs trailing, and feeds mostly on insects, though to a considerable extent on fish; also on reptiles and amphibians, crustaceans, arachnids and molluscs; very rarely birds and mammals. Individual as a rule. Voice croaking, guttural; sometimes a quack in flight.

DISTRIBUTION AND MOVEMENTS. A bird apparently confined to reed-beds, breeding (*I. m. minutus*) north to the Baltic shore, in Russia to the head-basins of the Volga, and the Khirgiz Steppes; east to Turkestan, Kashmir and the Indus in India; south to Persia, Iraq, Syria, Egypt, the Mediterranean, Tunis, Algeria and Morocco; west to Spain, France, Belgium and Holland: also *I. m. payesii*, S.W. Arabia and Africa south of the Sahara; *I. m. podiceps* Madagascar; *I. m. dubius* Australia;

I. m. novaezealandiae New Zealand. Birds breeding in Western Europe probably all winter to S. Africa; to Britain a wanderer at spring and autumn passage-time, most commonly in southeast England. Absolute proof lacking, but may have bred East Anglia and could easily do so unnoticed.

TO READ. F. Groebbels (1935). *Beobachtungen am Nest der Zwergrohrdommel* (Ixobrychus m. minutus *L.*). Journal für Ornithologie, vol. 83, pp. 525–51. O. Steinfatt (1935). *Beobachtungen und Betrachtungen am Nest der Zwergrohrdommel*. Beiträge zur Fortpflanzungsbiologie der Vögel, vol. 11, pp. 14–22, 51–58.

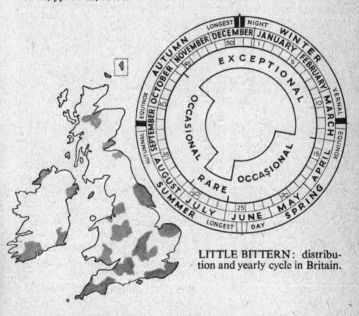

LITTLE BITTERN: distribution and yearly cycle in Britain.

BITTERN—*continued*

regular visitor to England, irregular in Scotland, mostly on passage; and in East Anglia a new breeding stock is gradually increasing and spreading; almost certainly extinct as a breeder between 1886 and 1911; formerly nested widely.

TO READ. Miss E. L. Turner (1911). *The return of the bittern to Norfolk*. British Birds, vol. 5, pp. 90–97. A. F. J. Portielje (1926). *Zur Ethologie bezw. Psychologie von* Botaurus stellaris (*L.*). Ardea, Leiden, vol. 15, pp. 1–15. R. Zimmermann (1931). *Zur Fortpflanzungsbiologie der grossen Rohrdommel*, Botaurus stellaris *L.* Journal für Ornithologie, vol. 79, pp. 324–32.

WHOOPER SWAN *Cygnus cygnus* (LINNAEUS, 1758)

WHOOPER SWAN, about 1/11 (see also p. 168)

RECOGNITION. Gigantic. Length about 5 ft., of which body about half. Weight, male 21-27 lbs:, female 18-19 lbs. White, cygnets greyish. Holds very long neck straighter and more upright than other swans. Yellow patch on bill (whitish in young) tapers from base to a point below nostril. Flight steady and direct, with neck straight out, whistling (not humming) sound of wings. Grazes under water and on land on grasses and water-plants, including water-crowfoot, white clover, cotton-grass, flote-grass and reed-poa. Social as a rule away from breeding-haunts. Voice 'hoop-ah'; other notes at breeding-place.

BREEDING. Individual. Display-ceremonies on water culminating in excited rising by male and female breast to breast. False drinking. Amongst noises is distinct cooing song by male. Nests built by female with water-plants brought by male, on island or by shore of lake in open country. Eggs 4 to 7, normally 5 or 6, laid at 2-day intervals, length 4¼ to 5 in., cream-white. Female alone incubates, beginning when clutch completed, for 5 or 6 weeks; both parents manage young until they fly in about 9 weeks. Nestling grey above, white below. Cygnet attains adult plumage in second season after that in which it is hatched.

DISTRIBUTION AND MOVEMENTS. A bird of northern open waters in Europe and Asia, breeding in Iceland and Scotland and probably north to Arctic Ocean from Norway, Sweden, Finland, Upper Volga, Kirghiz Steppes, Turkestan, Altai Mts., R. Amur, Japan, Kamchatka and Komandorski Is. European birds winter as far as N. Mediterranean and Black Sea. In Britain mainly a winter-visitor, common in Western Isles of Scotland; in England regular on coast but inland only in very hard weather. Breeds in Highlands, irregularly and desultorily.

TO READ. A. Gordon (1922). *Nesting of the whooper swan in Scotland*. British Birds, vol. 15, pp. 170–71. E. Christoleit (1926). *Bemerkungen zur Biologie der Schwäne*. Journal für Ornithologie, vol. 74, pp. 464–90.

Note: has also nested in West Highlands.

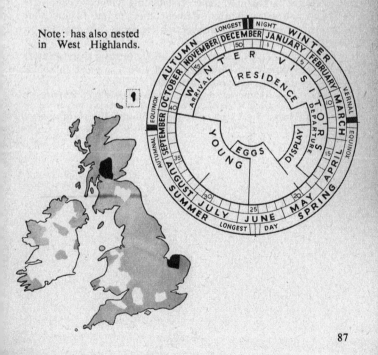

BEWICK'S SWAN   *Cygnus bewickii* YARRELL, 1830

RECOGNITION. Gigantic. Length about 4 ft., of which body about half. Weight 11-16 lbs. White, cygnets greyish. Neck relatively shorter than that of whooper, and not held quite so straight up, though not curved like mute's. Forward boundary of yellow patch on bill is semicircle *behind* nostril; very clear distinction from whooper. Flight like whooper; wing-beat more hurried, noticeable when birds flying together but perhaps not when alone. Grazes in water and on land on grasses and water-plants, mostly of naiad family (grass-wrack, horned and fennel pondweeds), but white clover also recorded. Like most swans and geese, has winter flocks in which each family unit is detectable. Individual at breeding-place. Voice 'hoo', but other notes, even a cooing song, have been heard away from breeding-place.

DISTRIBUTION AND MOVEMENTS. A bird of northern open waters in Europe and Asia, with a breeding-distribution restricted to the tundra-lands and Arctic islands and rivermouths of Russia and Siberia from the Kanin Peninsula in the west to the R. Kolyma and Sakhalin in the east, including Kolguev I. and part of Novaya Zemlya. Western elements migrate into N. and mid-Europe in winter, large numbers to Holland, fair numbers to England, Wales and Ireland, relatively fewer to Scotland. In hard winters when Zuyder Zee (where 2–3,000 normally spend winter) and other waters of Holland frozen, often a great influx in Britain, with other species of Anatidae.

TO READ. G. A. Brouwer and L. Tinbergen (1939). *De Verspreiding der kleine zwanen*, Cygnus b. bewickii *Yarr.*, *in de Zuider-zee, voor en na de verzoeting*. Limosa, vol. 12, pp. 1–18. H. F. Witherby (1939). *The influx of Bewick's and whooper swans, winter* 1938–9. British Birds, vol. 32, pp. 378–81

BEWICK'S SWAN, about 1/9 (see also p. 168)

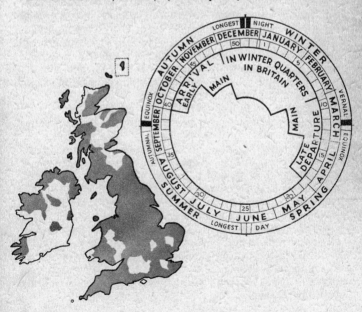

MUTE SWAN *Cygnus olor* (Gmelin, 1789)

RECOGNITION. Gigantic. Length about 5 ft., of which body about half. Weight 20 to 30 and possibly to 50 lbs. (may be heaviest flying bird). White, cygnets brownish (exceptionally white). Swims and walks with neck curved in S. Bill orange, not yellow, with base black and knob (absent on whooper and Bewick's) black. Flight steady and fast, with slow wing-beats and unique throbbing buzz. Grazes in water, but also on land, on water star-wort, grass-wrack, pondweed, arrowhead, water-thyme, grass, reeds, stonewort and other plants, and has been known to eat amphibians, fish, insects, molluscs and worms. Sociable; in Britain mostly family-groups. Voice very rare and mostly confined to nesting-territory (hisses and snorts and rare trumpeting note).

BREEDING. Individual and social. Can raise secondary wing-feathers to form near-tunnel over back, as threat to other species of animal. Display mutual breast-touching, neck-raising and snorting; also head-dipping, false preening and false feeding. Nests, large, built by female with sticks and water-plants brought by male, on island, by shore of lake or in bend or backwater of river. Eggs 5–9 ('domestic' birds 4–12), normally 6 or 7, usually laid on successive days, but sometimes at 2-day intervals, length 4¼ to 4¾ in., white, faintly turquoise. Female mostly, with male for short (but regular) spells, incubates for 5 or 6 weeks; both parents manage young which may not fly for 20 weeks. Nestling grey above, white below. Cygnet attains adult plumage in second season after that in which it is hatched.

DISTRIBUTION AND MOVEMENTS. A bird of calm estuaries and sea-lochs, lakes, ponds and slow rivers of north-central Europe and Asia, north to Shetland, Denmark, Sweden, E. Prussia, Poland, Russia in Europe to head-basins of Volga (*c.* 60° N.), Siberia to ? *c.* 55° N.; east to Pacific coast beyond R. Amur; south to Mongolia, Turkestan, N. Persia, Asia Minor, Rumania, Poland, N. Germany, Denmark and England; west to Ireland and Outer Hebrides. Breeds in other European countries as 'domestic' species. Large resident (breeding) communities at L. Takern in Sweden (up to 1,000 pairs), on most larger English rivers, Abbotsbury in Dorset (sometimes over 500 pairs), Loch Bee in South Uist, Outer Hebrides (*c.* 150 pairs) and other places. W. European birds migrate to C. Europe in winter; some may reach Britain but nearly all British birds strictly resident, moving only in hard weather.

MUTE SWAN, about 1/11 (see also p. 168)

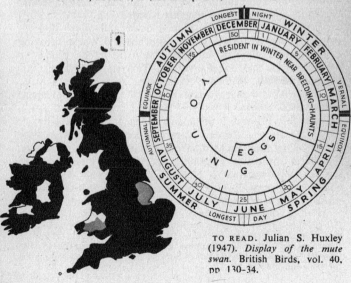

TO READ. Julian S. Huxley (1947). *Display of the mute swan*. British Birds, vol. 40, pp. 130–34.

GREY-LAG   *Anser anser* (LINNAEUS, 1758)

RECOGNITION. Very large. Length nearly 3 ft., of which body just under two-thirds. Weight 6½ to 9, av. 7½ lbs. Head large; same shade as body. Bill thick and longish, of adult wholly orange except for light tip. Leading part of upper wing and rump pale grey (these characters *not* very useful in flight); tail white with broad dark band near end. Breast plain (young) or spotted, not barred. Legs flesh-pink. Flight steady, fast, not heavy or clumsy in spite of weight of bird. Moves in groups from family-size to some thousands. Flies in regular V on long passages. Feeds by grazing on land and in water, on grasses, corn, legumes, potatoes, roots; also on cloud berries, acorns, duckweed, grass-wrack. Voice like farmyard goose (of which ancestor) but many variants.

BREEDING. Individual in Britain. Social displays of small parties; crouch, hiss. Courtship with head near ground, and honking. Nests usually in heather, built by goose of sticks, grasses and rushes, much of which brought by gander, lined down, often on islets or near shore of loch. Eggs 4–9, normally 5 or 6, laid daily, length 3 to 3¾ in., buff-white. Goose alone incubates *c.* 4 weeks, starting when clutch complete. Both tend young until they fly *c.* 8 weeks from hatching. Nestling brown and green-yellow. Young attain adult plumage in third, but may breed in second season after that in which they are hatched.

DISTRIBUTION. A bird of wild moor and marsh and (in winter) coastal pastures and saltings of the Old World, breeding n. to Iceland, Norway, Finland, Russia to *c.* 60° N.; e. to Manchuria; s. to Mongolia – Tibet – Turkestan – Afghanistan – Persia, Caucasus, Rumania, Macedonia, Yugo-Slavia, Austria, Czechoslovakia, N. Germany e. of the Elbe, and N. Highlands; w. to Outer Hebrides; has bred in Friesland (N.W. Germany), Vosges (N.E. France), S. Spain and L. Fazzara (N.E. Algeria).

MOVEMENTS. European elements nearly all move s. for winter, many reaching Mediterranean but none crossing Sahara. Iceland birds invade Highlands, W. Lowlands and Ireland; regular winter-visitors to N.W. England and N. Wales. Not common E. coast S. of Forth. The surviving British breeders mostly resident through the year near breeding-grounds.

TO READ. Chistoleit, see under white-front, p. 94. K. Lorenz and N. Tinbergen (1938). *Taxis und Instinkthandlung in der Eirollbewegung der Graugans, I.* Zeitschrift für Tierpsychologie, Berlin vol. 2, pp. 1–29. Papers by Berry, Beveridg, Coombes, Graham, Robinson and Smalley on *Changes in the distribution of British grey geese* in the Scottish Nauturalist for 1932 and 1933.

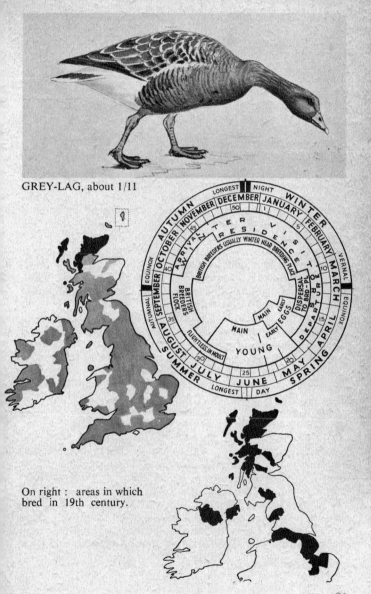

GREY-LAG, about 1/11

LONGEST NIGHT
WINTER
AUTUMN
OCTOBER NOVEMBER DECEMBER JANUARY FEBRUARY
SEPTEMBER
AUGUST
JULY
JUNE
MAY
APRIL
MARCH
SPRING
SUMMER
LONGEST DAY

ARRIVAL
WINTER VISIT
WINTER RESIDENCE
BRITISH BREEDERS USUALLY WINTER NEAR BREEDING PLACE
DEPARTURE
VERNAL EQUINOX
DISPERSAL TO BRD.-PL.
EARLY EGGS
MAIN
BRITISH BREEDERS FLOCK
FLIGHTLESS IN MOULT
MAIN
EARLY
YOUNG
AUTUMNAL EQUINOX

45
50
5
10
15
20
25
30
35
40

On right : areas in which
bred in 19th century.

WHITE-FRONT *Anser albifrons* (SCOPOLI, 1769)

RECOGNITION. Large. Length up to 2 ft. 6 in. of which body just under two-thirds. Weight gander 4½ to 7½ lbs., goose 4 to 6½ lbs. Head largish, but not as large as that of grey-lag; head and neck not darker than back (compare pink-foot). The darkest-coloured of the grey geese. Bill yellow (young), orange (N.W. Greenland adults) or pink (other adults) with white tip, not as long as grey-lag's but longer than pink-foot's. Fore-wing *not* paler than rest of wing. Tail white, broad dark band near end. Breast and under-parts plain (young), strongly barred with black (adult). Prominent white patch above bill of adult, but not young on which dark feathering at base of bill. Legs orange. Flight active and fast, the most manoeuvrable of the grey geese. V-formation on long passages. Feeds by grazing on grasses and corn; also recorded white clover, sea-lavender, sea-plantain, sea-arrow-grass, berries and water-insects. Voice an eerie high-pitched dog-like laughing, often uttered by gaggles high in flight.

DISTRIBUTION. A bird of tundra the summer, and in winter saltings, marshes, estuarine flats and meadows of Europe, Asia and North America. *A. a. albifrons* breeds all round Polar Basin, especially at mouths of its rivers, east along the Old World mainland from the Kanin Peninsula to Bering Straits (and on Kolguev Is., Novaya Zemlya and New Siberian Is.), and along New World mainland from Yukon Delta probably to Perry R. From the Perry R. probably to the Back R. and Melville Peninsula breeds *A. a. gambelli*, the larger but otherwise very similar Tule Goose. In N.W. and W. Greenland breeds an isolated population of orange-yellow-billed whitefronts now known as *A. a. flavirostris*. Does *not* breed in Iceland.

MOVEMENTS. Greenland breeders pass in autumn, probably *via* Iceland, to Ireland (some also Western Isles, W. Scotland and W. England, and a few to Gulf of St. Lawrence). Old World (pink-billed) breeders migrate to Britain, France, Mediterranean, Asia Minor, Persia, Himalayas, S. China, Japan; New World *albifrons* to Mexico and Caribbean; *gambelli* to Sacramento Valley, California. Pink-billed white-fronts (*albifrons*) winter regularly in Hebrides, N. Argyll, Solway, Norfolk and Severn-mouth, and pass through Shetland and Orkney and along both E. and W. coasts. Recently driven from only regular inland haunt (Nene Valley, Northants) by drainage of water-meadows.

WHITE-FRONT,
about 1/8

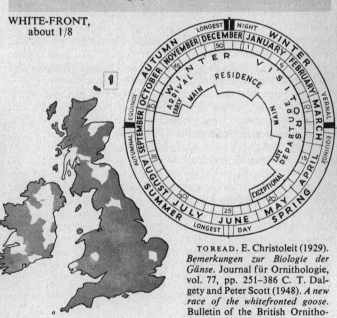

TO READ. E. Christoleit (1929). *Bemerkungen zur Biologie der Gänse.* Journal für Ornithologie, vol. 77, pp. 251–386 C. T. Dalgety and Peter Scott (1948). *A new race of the whitefronted goose.* Bulletin of the British Ornithologists' Club, vol. 68, pp. 109–21.

BEAN-GOOSE   *Anser arvensis arvensis* BREHM, 1831

RECOGNITION. Very large. Length 2 ft. 6 in. to nearly 3 ft., of which body just under two-thirds. Weight male 7–9½ lbs., female 6½–7½ lbs. Head and neck not noticeably darker than back (compare pink-foot). The brownest of the grey geese. Bill longer and heavier than that of other grey geese (not short and small as pink-foot), black with very variable amount of orange (young, yellow); always black tip. Fore-wing not noticeably paler than rest of wing. Tail white, broad dark band near end. Under-parts always plain. Sometimes white feathers at base of bill. Legs orange (young, yellow). Flight and habits much as other grey geese; does not flight so regularly between night- and day-grounds. Feeds by grazing on land, but also in water, on grasses; and on water-cress, clover, cotton-grass, marsh-horsetail, lichens and berries; eats also corn. Voice not often heard in flight, usually a low-pitched bleating.

DISTRIBUTION AND MOVEMENTS. A bird of the open northern forests and tundra in the summer, and perhaps more inland in winter than other grey geese. Species *Anser arvensis* breeds in Greenland and round Old World half of Polar Basin; *A. a. brachyrhynchus*, the pink-footed goose, on tundra of Iceland, N.E. Greenland, Spitsbergen and perhaps Franz Josef Land; *A. a. arvensis*, the bean-goose, north to Lapland, Kolguev Is., Novaya Zemlya and arctic coast Siberia, east to Taimyr Peninsula and upper Yenesei R., south into forest area to about 64° N. on E., about 58° N. west of Urals, about 63° N. in Lapland, about 61° N. in Norway; west to Norway. Further east in Asia the arctic tundra and rivermouths from the R. Lena to the Bering Straits are inhabited by *A. a. serrirostris*, and the northern forests east to Kamchatka, south to Mongolia and west to about the R. Irtish (Tomsk) by *A. a. middendorfi*. The bean-goose race migrates in winter as far as the N. Mediterranean, Asia Minor and Persia. In Britain regular resident winter flocks mainly in W. Lowlands, Northumberland and East Anglia; rare or irregular passenger elsewhere, except for odd birds sometimes attached to large flocks of other grey geese.

TO READ. E. Wibeck (1929). *Bidrag till kännedomen om sädgåsens* (Anser fabalis *Lath.*) *häckterräng i Sverige*. Fauna och Flora, Uppsala for 1929, pp. 206–15. G. P. Dementiew (1935). *Essai de revision des formes de l'oie des moissons* Anser fabalis *Latham*. Alauda, vol. 8, pp. 169–93. H. Johansen (1945). *Races of bean-geese*. Dansk ornithologisk Forenings Tidsskrift, vol. 39, pp. 106–27.

BEAN-GOOSE, about 1/8

PINK-FOOT *Anser arvensis brachyrhynchus* BAILLON, 1833

RECOGNITION. Large. Length 2 to 2½ ft., of which body about two-thirds. Weight 4 to 7½, av. 6½ lbs. Head and neck dark, noticeably in contrast with paler *bluish*-grey upper-parts of body of adult. Bill shorter, smaller and finer than bean's, black with pink band; black tip. Fore-wing sometimes, though not always, paler than rest of wing. Tail white, broad dark band near end. Under-parts plain, though those of young appear mottled. Sometimes (rare) a few white feathers at base of bill, but when present scarcely appreciable in field. Legs pink (young, yellow-flesh). Flight much as other geese. Flocks generally large, and regularly flight between night roosting-grounds (muds and sea-flats) and day (or moonlight) feeding grounds (meadows, etc.). Feeds by grazing, almost entirely on land, on grasses and corn-crops (stubbles and sprouting drills) in winter, also on potatoes; and on scurvy-grass, alpine mouse-ear chickweed, clover, trefoil, saxifrages, reticulate willow, horsetails and other available plants of tundra and meadow. Voice gaggling 'gugnunc', high (gander), low (goose).

DISTRIBUTION AND MOVEMENTS. Breeds on the tundra of north-east Greenland, mostly north of Scoresby Sound, where has probably been increasing; in the oases in the central desert of Iceland, where has certainly been increasing in last twenty-five years; and on the coastal tundra of Spitsbergen and probably of Franz Josef Land. Most of the world population on its way south makes its landfall near Strathy Point in N. Sutherland, quickly crosses along Caithness border to the sandy firths of the east coast, and passes on to form regular resident winter communities in the open estuaries, marshes, cultivated valleys and hills of the west and south shores of the North Sea (Britain, Belgium, Holland and Germany; rarely France). In Britain winter flocks on east coast from Easter Ross to Norfolk; and on west some in Inner Hebrides, Clyde, Solway, Lancs., and Severn. Some of these larger west coast flocks, e.g. Solway, may move over to E. coast in or after late autumn. Rare elsewhere; only fourteen Irish records to 1941 recorded in *Handbook*.

TO READ. Dementiew and Johansen, see under bean-goose. W. Maitland Congreve and S. W. P. Freme (1930). *Seven weeks in eastern and northern Iceland.* Ibis, series 12, vol. 6, pp. 193–228 (esp. 204–18). G. Timmermann (1933). *Die Kurzschnabelgans in Island.* Journal für Ornithologie, Berlin, vol. 81, pp. 322–30. John Berry (1939). *International wildfowl inquiry, volume II, The status and distribution of wild geese and wild duck in Scotland.* Cambridge, University Press, pp. 33–40.

PINK-FOOT, about 1/8

BARNACLE-GOOSE   *Branta leucopsis* (BECHSTEIN, 1803)

RECOGNITION. Medium-large. Length about 2 ft. (male larger than female), of which body about three-quarters. Weight $2\frac{1}{2}$ to 6 lbs., av. 4 lbs., gander usually heavier than goose. The most pied of the black geese. Head, neck and breast black, with whole face and forehead creamy-white (black line joins bill to eye) or dusky-white (young). Upper-parts grey with thin black and white bars, rump white, tail black; wing-ends black. Under-parts pale grey, white under tail. Bill short and thin, black. Legs and feet black. Flight lighter than grey geese, but much more of a goose-type than of duck-type; fast. Flocks often fairly large, but not thousands; winters on coastal pastures on which may stay day and night if undisturbed. Feeds in Britain almost entirely on grasses; also creeping buttercup, marsh-marigold, white clover, procumbent celery, daisy, grass-wrack, marsh-horsetail, sea-weed, moss and liverwort; in breeding-haunts grasses, mountain-sorrel, arctic willow, etc. Voice in packs yelping barks.

DISTRIBUTION AND MOVEMENTS. Known (so far) to breed only in N.E. Greenland, Spitsbergen and Novaya Zemlya (nests on cliff-ledges); passes through Iceland-Faeroe and Lapland-Scandinavia to winter in Britain and on or near shores of North Sea and Baltic. Vagrant in other parts of Europe and to E. North America. In Britain winters in numbers in Hebrides; in fair numbers in N. and N.W. Ireland; in (reduced) numbers Solway; in small (but increasing ?) numbers (usually attached to pink-foot flocks) east Scotland and S.E. Ireland; elsewhere coastal passenger and irregular visitor.

TO READ. A. L. V. Manniche (1910). *The terrestrial mammals and birds of north-east Greenland; biological observations. Danmark-Expedition til Grønlands Nordøstkyst* 1906–1908. Meddelelser om Grønland, vol. 45, pp. 1–200 (first discovery of nest in G., June 1908). A. Koenig (1911). *Avifauna Spitzbergensis.* Bonn, pp. 222–26 (first discovery of nest in S., 29 June 1907). F. C. R. Jourdain (1922). *The breeding habits of the barnacle goose.* Auk, vol. 39, pp. 166–71.

BARNACLE-GOOSE,
about 1/7 (see also p. 169).

BRENT GOOSE   *Branta bernicla* (LINNAEUS, 1758)

BRANT, or BLACK BRANT in North America.

RECOGNITION. Medium-large. Length up to 2 ft., of which head and neck 6 in. or more. Weight gander 2¾ to 4½ lbs., goose 2¼ to 3¾ lbs. The smallest British goose. Head, neck and breast black with (adults only) small white patch on sides of neck. Upper-parts slate-grey (dark-bellied race) or brownish-grey (light-bellied race); immatures only have narrow pale edges to feathers of back; rump white, tail black; wings dark, faint white lines on inner part (immatures only); under-parts slate-grey on dark-bellied race and whitish-grey on light-bellied race; under-tail white. Bill, legs and feet black; bill longer than barnacle's. Flight more like large duck's than other geese; fast. Flocks often rather irregular in flight; occasionally over a thousand. The most marine of the geese; normally restricted in winter to the world between tides. Used to feed in winter-range almost entirely on the inter-tidal grass-wrack, *Zostera*; this has widely disappeared from N. Atlantic coasts in present century; brent is changing to green sea-weeds *Enteromorpha* and *Ulva* (sea-lettuce) and other plants. Also eats grass, buttercups, mouse-ear chickweed, saxifrages, mountain-sorrel, cotton-grass, other sea-weeds, mosses, crusta-ceans and molluscs, most of these on breeding-grounds. Voice a gabbling grunting, 'rott . . rott. . ', 'grrr . . hronk', 'ruk . . runk'.

DISTRIBUTION AND MOVEMENTS. A bird of the river mouths and islands of the Polar Basin in the breeding-season, and of the coastal flats of temperate Europe, Asia and N. America in the winter. Breeding range is *Branta bernicla bernicla*, the dark-bellied brent, Kolguev-Novaya Zemlya-Waigatz-Yalmal-Taimyr; *B. b. nigricans*, the black brent, Taimyr-New Siberian Is. – N. Siberia – Bering Straits – MacKenzie – Coronation Gulf – W. Victoria I. – Banks and Melville Is.; *B. b. hrota*, the American brent, or light-bellied brent, Boothia Peninsula – North Somerset, Corn-wallis, Devon, Axel Heiberg and Ellesmere Islands – N. Green-land – Spitsbergen-Franz Josef Land. In Europe light-bellied brent winters s. to English Channel and s. North Sea; dark-bellied brent to same, but also to Baltic and Iberian Peninsula. In Britain flocks inhabit all suitable coastal flats. Light-bellied brents are found from the Moray Firth n., w. and s. to S.W. Britain, almost purely through Hebrides and in Clyde, and predominantly in Ireland, W. England and Wales. Brents are almost purely of dark-bellied form from Firth of Tay s. and w. to Dorset; late in winter season some dark birds appear to penetrate west.

BRENT GOOSE, about 1/10 (see also p. 169)
Left: adult dark-bellied; right: immature light-bellied

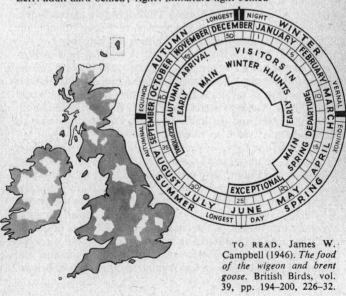

TO READ. James W. Campbell (1946). *The food of the wigeon and brent goose*. British Birds, vol. 39, pp. 194–200, 226–32.

CANADA GOOSE *Branta canadensis* (LINNAEUS, 1758)

RECOGNITION. Immense. Length 3 ft. or more, of which body about three-fifths. Gander (6¼–13½ lbs., av. 8½) on average larger than goose (5¼ to 13 lbs., av. 7). The largest goose in Britain. Head and neck black with prominent white patch from chin to behind eye, on some divided under chin by black mid-line. Tail black, upper-tail and under-tail pure white, rest of body including wings and upper-breast brown, very light brown to white underneath (looks grey in flight). Bill, legs and feet black. Flight fast, wing-beats steady, in V's or lines on passages; social in winter, all local families flock together. Feeds by grazing on grasses and water-plants; also on grass-wrack, various seaweeds including sea-lettuce, insects, crustaceans, molluscs and worms. Voice 'ah'onk', very loud and penetrating.

BREEDING. Individual. Probably pairs for life. Ganders drive other ganders from neighbourhood of goose with bows, wing-flaps and hisses, and return to mutual neck-snaking ceremony. Nests in Britain usually on islets in fresh waters, of sticks, grasses and rushes lined down. Eggs 4–11, usually 5 or 6, length 3¼ in. to 3¾ in., cream-white. Goose only incubates for about 4 weeks and tends young until they fly in about 6 weeks. Gander stands guard on nest territory and brood. Gosling yellow; green-brown on top of head and neck and on upper-parts. Young attains adult plumage in first season after that in which it is hatched.

DISTRIBUTION AND MOVEMENTS. A resident bird in Britain, where introduced from N. America many times from the seventeenth century onwards, and now established wild. Natural breeding-range of species is north to arctic shore of New World mainland, S. Victoria Island, Boothia Peninsula, S. Cockburn Land and Fox Land (in Baffin Island) and Labrador; east to Newfoundland; south to Magdalen Islands, and to about lat. 50° N. in Quebec, to N.E. Ontario, Manitoba, Minnesota, N. and S. Dakota, Nebraska and to about lat. 40° N. in Colorado and states west (not California); west to Nevada, Oregon, Washington and Pacific Ocean, Commander Is., Kurile Is., Kamchatka and E. end of Siberia. Divided in N. America into eight subspecies, of which *B. c. canadensis*, Newfoundland-Labrador, the race introduced to Britain, is the largest. This still breeds in Britain much in protected parkland and on large estates, but disperses in winter regularly over many parts of midland, eastern and southern England; rarer, or less regular, in other parts of Britain.

CANADA GOOSE, about 1/9 (see also p. 169)

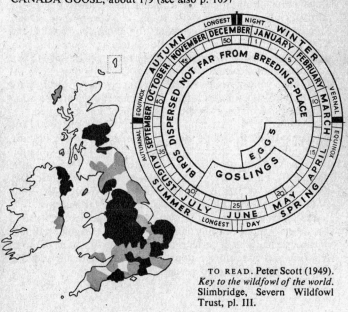

TO READ. Peter Scott (1949). *Key to the wildfowl of the world.* Slimbridge, Severn Wildfowl Trust, pl. III.

SHELDUCK *Tadorna tadorna* (LINNAEUS, 1758)

RECOGNITION. Medium-large. Length about 2 ft., of which body about two-thirds. Weight 1¼ to 3¼ lbs. A very goose-like duck, with an unique pattern of red, pink, chestnut, green-black and white. Sexes alike. Head and neck black shot green; body white with broad hoop of chestnut round breast and front of back, and black on sides of back (scapulars), darkish down mid-line of under-parts; in flight leading half of inner wing white, trailing half dark; speculum (see p. 16) green, chestnut above; wing-ends black. Tail white, extreme tip black; under-tail chest-nut. Bill red (male has knob), legs and feet pink. Flight rather slow; goose-like; feeds usually in packs mainly on the molluscs of sand and mud; on fish, insects, crustaceans and worms; and on sea-weed, grasses and water-plants. Voice 'ag-ag-ag', like a laugh in falling cadence; other notes at breeding-place.

BREEDING. Individual. Displays aggressive (drake-drake) and mutual (drake-duck), mostly involve stretching and curving of neck, with bowing, whistling and clucking. Nests within a few miles of coast, usually in deep rabbit-burrows in dunes but often under cover on moorland or farmland, lined down. Eggs 7–20, normally about 10, length 2½ to 2¾ in., cream-white. Duck, assisted partly by drake, incubates for about four weeks, and takes young to water not long after hatching, where may pool them in nurseries. Drake guards nest-territory and passage to sea. Young fly about 8 weeks after hatching. Duckling brown (almost black) and white; white under-parts; upper-parts mostly dark brown, but white forehead, face and rump. Young attains adult plumage in second season after that in which it is hatched.

DISTRIBUTION. Coastal flats and estuaries of temperate and temperate-tropical Europe, and inland seas and waters of Asia, breeding (*a*) round shores of Britain, N. Sea, Norway, Baltic; (*b*) in W. Mediterranean from Sardinia to S. Spain, S. France and Algeria (L. Fazzara) (*c*) from Aegean and Black Seas into Asia (Iraq – Persia – Caspian – Aral – Turkestan – Tibet – Mongolia – Manchuria n. into Siberia). British breeders increasing.

MOVEMENTS. Nearly all British breeders, and others in group (*a*) desert young in July and migrate to Heligoland Bight, whence gradually return after moulting. Some passage movements in spring and late summer along coasts and, increasingly, along inland waterways and to sewage farms, etc.

SHELDUCK, about 1/8

TO READ. Henry Boase (1935, 38). *On the . . . . habits of the shelduck.* British Birds, vol. 28, pp. 218–24, vol. 31, p. 367–71. J. Hoogerheide and W. K. Kraak (1942). *Voorkomen en trek van de bergeend.* Ardea, Leiden, vol. 31, pp.1 -19. R.A.H. Coombes (1950). *The moult migration of the shelduck.* Ibis, vol. 92, pp. 405-18.

MALLARD   *Anas platyrhyncha* LINNAEUS, 1758

RECOGNITION. Medium-large. Length nearly 2 ft. of which body about two-thirds. Weight drake 2–3½, duck 1¾–3 lbs. Closely resembles some domestic ducks, of which it is the ancestor. Both sexes have a brown fore-wing (i.e. leading half of inner half), a speculum (see p. 16) which is purple with black above and white bars fore and aft; and orange legs and feet. Drake has metallic green head and neck, with a white neck-ring below (prominent), grey back and belly (back brown in middle), purple-brown breast, green-yellow bill. Duck is mottled brown; bill dark olive, orange at sides. In late summer drake goes into duck-like eclipse plumage. Flight fast with typical harsh whispering whistling. Feeds often in flocks by night and day by dabbling, up-ending and grazing; in Britain on polygonum, persicaria, sedges and grasses; on crowfoot, blackberry, bedstraw, seablite, hornwort, water-starwort, acorns, duckweed, grass-wrack, pondweed, and corn; and on amphibians, small fish, insects, crustaceans and worms (animal element *c.* 10% by vol.). Voice of duck a gross farmyard quack, of drake lower, more repetitive quacking, also high short whistle during display.

BREEDING. Individual. Displays include 'crowding' duck, bobbing, bowing, water-flicking, neck-stretching, and pursuit-flights of duck by drakes. Nest in almost any cover near water, often at the tops of trees, site chosen and lined by duck with grass and down. Eggs 6–16, normally about 10, laid daily, length about 2¼ in., turquoise-buff. Duck only incubates, starting on full clutch, for 3½ to 4½ weeks, takes ducklings to water when dry; they can fly after 7 or 8 weeks. Drake guards nesting-territory, and may sometimes help to manage young. Duckling yellow-buff below, dark olive-brown above, with pair of roundish yellow patches on back and another pair on rump; face buff with dark line 'through' eye and dark streak below. Young attains adult plumage in first season after that in which it is hatched.

DISTRIBUTION. Almost every sort of marsh and water-side, breeding through the world from latitude 30–35° N. to forest-line, and beyond it in Alaska, Greenland, Iceland and N. Europe; within this range absent as breeder only from S. Japan, S.E. and Atlantic U.S., and from N.E. Ontario, Quebec, Labrador and Newfoundland. Breeds in Azores and in S. Greenland, where separated as *A. p. conboschas*. Some elements migrate, though not south of 20° N. except in E. Indies, where may reach Equator in Borneo.

MALLARD, drake and duck, about 1/8 (see also p. 170)

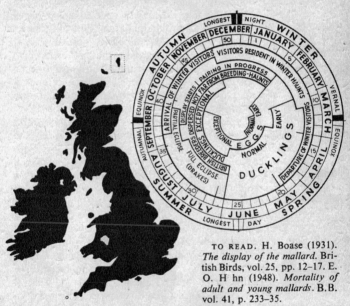

TO READ. H. Boase (1931). *The display of the mallard.* British Birds, vol. 25, pp. 12–17. E. O. H hn (1948). *Mortality of adult and young mallards.* B.B. vol. 41, p. 233–35.

MOVEMENTS. British breeders normally disperse, do not migrate. Birds from Baltic and other North Sea countries and Iceland-Faeroe, pass in spring and autumn on all coasts and many inland waters; few winter beyond England. Some individual birds may move differently in different years, probably under the influence of new companions.

GADWALL   *Anas strepera* LINNAEUS, 1758

RECOGNITION. Medium. Length about 20 in., of which body about two-thirds. Weight drake 25–41 oz., duck 21–36 oz. Both sexes have heads brown; fore-wing grey with chestnut patch (compare mallard), speculum (see p. 16) white with dark below and broad black bar forward, forming a square white patch on trailing edge of wing, best recognition character. Wings more pointed than mallard's. Legs and feet dull orange-yellow. Adults have white under-parts. Drake has dark grey bill; dark crescent markings on breast; vermiculated grey back; rump and upper-tail dense blue-black; under-tail black, neighbouring area of under-parts grey. Duck has grey bill with more orange at sides than duck mallard's; breast dark brown; is more slender than mallard and further distinguished by white under-parts. Drake in eclipse like duck, young like duck with spotted under-parts. Wing-beats, but not flight, faster than mallard's. Whistling lower. Feeds (in small flocks usually) by dabbling, up-ending and grazing, on pondweed, grasses, sedges and rushes; also eats corn, rice in India, algae and arrowheads; and amphibians, fish, insects, molluscs and worms (animal matter only 2%). Voice of duck a quack (higher than mallard's); of drake very low but penetrating 'krek', also whistle in display.

BREEDING. Individual. Display includes bowing, bobbing and pursuit-flights like mallard's. Nests under cover near water, site chosen and lined by duck with grass and down. Eggs 7–13, normally about 10, laid daily, length 2 to 2¼ in., buff-white. Duck only incubates, starting on full clutch, for about 4 weeks, takes ducklings to water when dry. Young fly at 7 weeks. Drakes show no interest in nest-territory or brood. Duckling very like mallard's, but lighter buff, dark line 'through' eye thinner and curves to back of crown, no dark streak below. Young attains adult plumage in first season after that in which it is hatched.

DISTRIBUTION. Sheltered inland waters, breeding in Old and New World between about 35° and 60° N., and in Iceland. In Old World breeding-range n. to Iceland, Sutherland, Central Sweden and 60° N. across Russia and Siberia; e. to Kamchatka and Commander Is.; s. to Mongolia, Turkestan, N. Afghanistan and Persia, Caucasus, Black Sea, Balkans (not Greece), Austria, ? N. Italy, Czechoslovakia, Germany, Holland and S.E. England, with outposts in S. France, N.E. Algeria and S. Spain; w. to Ireland. In New World n. perhaps to 60° N.; e. to Manitoba,

GADWALL, duck and drake, about 1/9 (see also p. 172)

Note: breeding irregular in
all black areas save Norfolk
and Kinross.

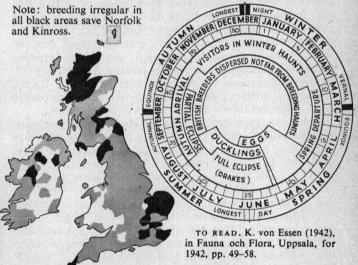

TO READ. K. von Essen (1942),
in Fauna och Flora, Uppsala, for
1942, pp. 49–58.

Ls. Superior and Michigan; s. to about 40° N.; w. to Pacific
States and S.E. Brit. Columbia. Old World birds migrate almost
to Equator in Asia and Africa, but New World birds not beyond
Caribbean.

MOVEMENTS. British breeders have been increasing for nearly
fifty years: resident and dispersive. Iceland birds visit Britain,
recent increases in winter visitors (especially to Inner Hebrides
and Ireland) reflecting increase of breeders in that country. Except
in west, autumn and spring movements slight and irregular.

111

TEAL *Anas crecca* LINNAEUS, 1758

EUROPEAN TEAL, and GREEN-WINGED TEAL, in N. America.

RECOGNITION. Small-medium. Length about 14 in., of which body about three-quarters. Weight 9 to 15 oz., av. 12. The smallest British duck. Both sexes have grey bill and legs, brown fore-wing, and main part of speculum (see p. 16) green and black. Drake has chestnut head with a green band with buff border from round eye to back of neck; back vermiculated grey with noticeable longitudinal white streak underlined with black; breast boldly marked small dark spots; belly white; under-tail black with conspicuous yellow-buff patches at sides; speculum green, black below, buff bar forward, faint white bar aft. Duck has head brown and white, little trace of eyestripe; back brown; under-parts white spotted brown; speculum green, black below, white bars fore and aft. Drakes in eclipse and 'of the year' like ducks. Flight the most acrobatic of the British ducks, fast and low with sudden swishing slides and turns. Feeds by grazing, picking, dabbling and up-ending, on sedges, pondweed, and grasses including *Panicum* and fescue; on many other plants and on animals (9% by vol. green-winged t.), including dead fish, frogs, insects, crustaceans, molluscs, worms. Voice of duck high-pitched quack, and inquisitive 'ek-ek'; of drake, short whistle.

BREEDING. Individual. Bowing and bobbing display on water of drakes round duck and pursuit-flights. Nests under cover, often in woodland or moorland, chosen and lined by duck with leaves and down. Eggs 6–?18, normally about 10, laid daily, length $1\frac{3}{4}$ to 2 in., buff, faintly green. Duck alone incubates, starting on full clutch, for 3 to $3\frac{1}{2}$ weeks. Takes young to water when dry; they fly after $3\frac{1}{2}$ weeks. Drake guards territory. Duckling like mallard's (smaller), has lower face-stripe. Young attains adult plumage in first season after that in which it is hatched.

DISTRIBUTION. Almost every sort of marsh, bog or waterside, breeding in the Old and New Worlds between 35° and 70° N. In Old World *A. c. crecca*, the 'European' teal, breeds n. to Iceland, in Europe and Siberia to the forest-line and in places beyond it; e. to Kamchatka, Kuriles, N. Japan, and N.E. China; s. to c. lat. 35° N. west to Turkestan, and to Transcaspia, Caucasus, Rumania, Yugoslavia, N. Italy, Sardinia and S. France; w. to France and Britain; irregular and exceptional breeder in Spain, Portugal, Azores, S. Greenland and Spitsbergen. In N. America replaced by green-winged teal, *A. c. carolinensis*, and by *A. c.*

TEAL, duck and drake, about 1/7 (see also p. 171)

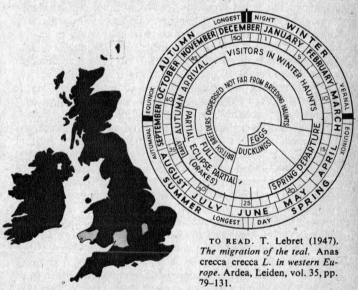

TO READ. T. Lebret (1947). *The migration of the teal.* Anas crecca crecca L. in western Europe. Ardea, Leiden, vol. 35, pp. 79–131.

nimea in Aleutians. Old World teal migrates nearly to equator in Africa and Asia; New World teal to Caribbean.

MOVEMENTS. British breeders resident and dispersive; normally migrate south only in hard winters. British Isles are invaded (mainly east coast) every autumn by a large number of teal which have bred mostly in Baltic and N. Sea countries, also in Iceland; many birds reach Ireland or go on to France and N. Spain. Return passage by same routes. Some individual birds move differently in different years.

GARGANEY   *Anas querquedula* LINNAEUS, 1758

RECOGNITION. Small-medium. Length about 15 in., of which body about two-thirds. Weight drake 10–16 oz., duck 9–14 oz. Practically as small as teal. Both sexes have grey legs, dark brown back and white-and-brown under-tail. Drake has black bill; head rich brown with fairly broad white band curving from above eye to back of neck; breast gold-brown with fine crescent-marking, contrasts sharply with very pale grey flanks; fore-wing blue-grey (important character); speculum (see p. 16) green, white bars fore and aft, when wing folded is overhung by long mantle feathers to form cross-pattern of blue-grey, white and black. Duck has green-grey bill; head brown and white with more distinct eye-stripe than duck teal; speculum very faint, greenish, white bars fore and aft, no mantle-feathers to overhang. Drake in eclipse keeps wing-pattern, otherwise as duck; juveniles much as duck. Flight fast, but does not jink like teal. Feeds (mostly in families, sometimes in flocks), by grazing, dabbling and darting, on crow-foot, white water-lily, dock, *Polygonum*, bur-reed, duckweed, pondweed, *Juncus* rush, sedge, *Glyceria* grass, *Phragmites* reed and sea-weed; probably eats more animal-matter than any British surface-feeding duck except shoveler, including fish, frogs, insects, crustaceans, molluscs and worms. Voice of drake a rattling 'klerrreb' like winding of fishing-reel, of duck 'knak', 'jack'.

BREEDING. Individual. Display bowing and bobbing on water of drake round duck, and pursuit-flights. Nests usually in grass or rushes, site chosen and lined by duck with grass and down. Eggs 6–14, normally about 10, laid daily, length 1½ to 2 in., cream-buff. Duck alone incubates, starting on full clutch, for 3 to 3½ weeks; takes young to water when dry; they fly after uncertain period, probably about 3½ weeks. Drake guards nest-territory but apparently not brood. Duckling can be distinguished from teal's because lower face-stripe is connected with upper by line in front of eye. Young attains adult plumage in second season after that in which it is hatched.

DISTRIBUTION AND MOVEMENTS. A bird of reedy waters in grassland, breeding through the Old World, north to S.E. England, to 61° N. in Sweden (not Norway), to 65° in Finland, to White Sea and Arctic Circle in Russia-in-Europe, to 55° N. on R. Yenesei and 62° N. on R. Lena; east to Kamchatka and N. Japan; south to Manchuria, Mongolia, ? Tibet, Turkestan, Caspian, Caucasus, ? N. Asia Minor, Bulgaria, Albania, C. Italy,

GARGANEY, drake and duck, about 1/6 (see also p. 171)

Note: Breeding irregular
except in S.E. England.

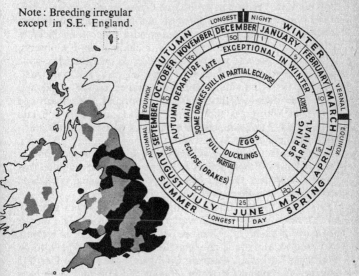

Tunisia, Sardinia and Pyrenees; west to France and England;
with an outpost breeding-population in Iceland, and others
(irregular) in S. Spain (Guadalquivir), Aegean (Naxos), Cyprus,
W. and N. England and Wales, E. Lowlands (increasing in
Britain). Migrates to Africa and Asia, in places somewhat beyond
Equator; recorded in Australia. From Britain entirely departs in
winter, and passengers seen fairly regularly on usual migration
routes in England; rare in Scotland and very rare in Ireland.

WIGEON *Anas penelope* LINNAEUS, 1758

EUROPEAN WIDGEON in North America.

RECOGNITION. Medium. Length about 18 in., of which body two-thirds. Weight drake 19–34 (? 38) oz., duck 16–28 (? 34) oz. Bill shorter and smaller than that of other surface-feeders, blue-grey with black tip; legs grey-brown; belly white, rather conspicuous in flight. Male has head chestnut with forehead and crown yellow-buff; in adult male broad white patch on fore-wing; speculum (see p. 16) green, white above, black bars fore and aft; under-tail black, contrasts boldly with white under-parts. Duck has head pink-buff spotted brown; fore-wing grey-brown; speculum dusky, or faintly green, conspicuous white bar forward, white bar aft. Young and drake in eclipse like duck but drake keeps wing-pattern. Flight of pack fairly fast and straight, hissing, wings look pointed. Feeds usually in large flocks, by grazing and dabbling, formerly mainly on *Zostera*, but now mainly on sedges, grasses, the naiad *Ruppia* and sea-weeds; other food includes many plants; a little animal matter including fish-fry, insects, spiders, molluscs and worms. Voice of drake whistle 'whee-you; whee-u-wheeee-you'; of duck a growling 'rak, rak, rak, rak'.

BREEDING. Individual. On water drakes 'crowd' ducks and bow; in air pursuit-flights. Nests on moorland, site chosen and lined duck with grass and down. Eggs 4–11, normally *c.* 8, laid daily, length 2 to 2¼ in., cream-buff. Duck alone incubates, starting on full clutch for 3½ to 4 weeks; young fly after *c.* 6 weeks. Drake guards territory and brood. Duckling more reddish-buff than mallard's. Young attains adult plumage in first year after that in which hatched; though drake gets no white wing-patch until second year, can breed without.

DISTRIBUTION. Tundra, moors and open woods in summer, and estuaries, flats, floods in winter, breeding through Old World, not s. of about 50° N. in Europe or 40° N. in Asia, n. to Iceland, and tundras and arctic river-mouths e. to Kamchatka; s. to N. Mongolia, Turkestan, Caspian, Caucasus, upper Volga, Don and Dneiper, N. Poland, Germany, Holland and England; w. to N.E. Ireland and Hebrides. Has also bred Greenland and Syria. Winters to Equator. In Britain first bred Sutherland 1849; spread, helped by introductions.

MOVEMENTS. Some British breeders migrate to Ireland or N.W. Europe, others winter in Britain. One was recovered in Iceland. Highlands and Islands, and whole E. coast, invaded in autumn by birds from Iceland, Baltic countries and Russia, which pass to S. and W., some going on to France and Iberian Peninsula.

WIGEON, duck and drake, about 1/7 (see also p. 170)

Note: breeding sporadic outside Highlands, and some colonized areas not now occupied.

The food of the wigeon, Mareca penelope Linn. Ibis, vol. 85, pp. 82–87; and see under brent goose, p. 102.

TO READ. W. E. Glegg (1943).

Black: breeding range before 1837; dark grey: colonized 1837-65; medium grey: 1866-94; light grey: 1895 and after.

117

PINTAIL *Anas acuta* LINNAEUS, 1758

RECOGNITION. Medium-large. Length including tail-feathers 25–29 in.; without them about 21–23 in., of which body about three-quarters. Weight drake 25–44 oz., av. 34 oz., duck 21–38 oz., av. 29 oz. Long slender neck; pointed tail and wings; bill and legs grey; white bar aft of speculum forms light trailing edge of wing. Drake has chocolate head, with white band down side of neck broadening into white breast; fore-wing and back mouse-grey; speculum (see p. 16) not very prominent, green, glossed with bronze-pink, black above, buff bar forward, white bar aft; belly white; under-tail black, contrasts boldly with neighbouring yellow patches on under-parts. General aspect drake very grey and white; white breast stands out when on water. Duck has brown head; brown fore-wing; speculum bronze-brown with only trace of green, white bar aft; belly spotted brown. Drake in eclipse and young like duck. Flight faster than wigeon's, continuous hissing. Feeds individually or in small flocks, by dabbling, up-ending and grazing, mostly on pondweed, sedges and grasses; and on many other plants; animal matter (America) 13% by vol.; includes frogs, fish, insects, crustaceans, molluscs and worms. Usually silent except at breeding-haunts; drake has teal-like whistle but a fifth lower; duck a 'quack' and a gruff 'krokrokro'.

BREEDING. Individual. Usual crowding of duck by drakes on water, bowing, bobbing, chasing; pursuit-flight of duck by drakes. Nests usually on islands in largish lakes, not always under cover, site chosen and lined by duck with down. Eggs 6–12, normally about 8, laid daily, length 2 to $2\frac{1}{2}$ in., yellowish-buff. Duck alone incubates, starting on full clutch, 3 to $3\frac{1}{2}$ weeks; young fly after about 7 weeks. Drake guards nest-territory. Duckling somewhat like mallard's but under-parts grey-white, not buff. Young attains adult plumage in first season after that in which hatched.

DISTRIBUTION. Tundra, moorland and cultivated land near largish lakes, and estuaries, flats and inland waters in winter, breeding in Old and New Worlds, not far south of 40° N. in America, Europe and W. Asia, or of 50° N. in E. Asia. In Old World breeds n. to Iceland, Lapland, coastal tundra and arctic river-mouths of Russia and Siberia; e. to Kamchatka ; s. to R. Amur, Baikal area, Atlas Mts., Turkestan, Caspian, Caucasus, Black Sea, Rumania, Hungary, Austria, Germany, S. France; w. to central France, England, N.E. Ireland, Hebrides, Faeroe and Iceland ; also S. Spain; may breed in Commander and Kurile Is.; and has bred in Spitsbergen. In New World breeds n. to

PINTAIL, drake and duck, about 1/8 (see also p. 171)

Note: breeding sporadic outside N. E. Highlands.

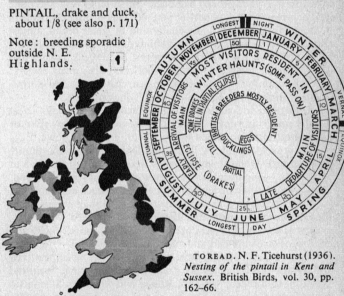

TO READ. N. F. Ticehurst (1936). *Nesting of the pintail in Kent and Sussex*. British Birds, vol. 30, pp. 162–66.

Arctic Ocean and Barren Lands; e. to Manitoba – Minnesota – Iowa; s. to c. lat. 40°N., w. into Pacific States, Brit. Columbia and Alaska. Old World race migrates in Africa to Abyssinia, and to equator in E. Indies; New World race to Caribbean, Hawaii.

MOVEMENTS. British breeders probably resident in winter. Small invasion of e. coast autumn by birds breeding in Iceland-Baltic and N. Sea areas, and even in W. Siberia and central Russia; passes by usual routes to w. including Ireland.

SHOVELER *Spatula clypeata* (Linnaeus, 1758)

RECOGNITION. Medium. Length about 20 in., of which body about three-fifths. Weight drake 16–31 oz., av. 23 oz., duck 16–26 oz., av. 20 oz. Both sexes sit squat, bill down, tail up; have large, spoon-shaped bill; blue fore-wing; green speculum (see p. 16) with broad white bar forward and narrow white bar aft; orange-red legs and feet. Drake a very pied bird, almost unmistakable; belly and flanks chestnut; bill black; head wholly dark green; breast white (no collar as mallard); back dark brown. Duck has belly and breast brown and pink-buff; bill green-brown with yellow at sides and lower mandible dull orange; but distinguished from other ducks by attitude and size of bill. Drake in eclipse and young much like duck. Flight fairly fast, and quite active; wings drum uniquely at take-off. Heavy bill noticeable in flight. In Britain feeds individually and in small flocks, almost entirely in water and marsh, by dabbling and up-ending. Vegetable foods (2/3 total vol.) are chiefly sedges, pondweeds, grasses and algae. Animal foods (1/3) chiefly molluscs; also many insects; and fish, amphibian tadpoles and spawn, crustaceans and worms. Voice of drake quiet 'took-took-took'; duck quacks.

BREEDING. Individual. Usual surface-feeder displays. Nest usually under fair cover in moor or pasture near slow river or lake. Site chosen and lined by duck with grass and down. Eggs 6–14, normally about 11, laid daily, length 2 to 2¼ in., faintly greenish-buff. Duck alone incubates, starting on full clutch, 3 to 3½ weeks; young fly after *c.* 6 weeks. Drake may guard brood. Duckling very like mallard's, but patches on back and rump not so clear; beak soon becomes distinctive. Young attains adult plumage in first season after that in which hatched.

DISTRIBUTION. Typical of many ducks, this pond, marsh and creek species of the Old and New Worlds has a main definable breeding-range, at considerable distances outside which scattered and erratic breeding has been recorded. Main range is in old World n. to Sweden, Finland, Russia and 70° N. in Siberia (in places further); e. to R. Kolyma and Maritime Province USSR; s. to line Baikal – Altai – Aral – Caspian, Caucasus, Black Sea, Macedonia, Yugoslavia, Austria, Germany, France; w. to Ireland and Hebrides. Outside records, not all erratic, are ? Kamchatka, Commander Is., N. Japan, ? N. Mongolia, ? Asia Minor, ? Cyprus, Switzerland, Corsica, S. Spain. Recently established as breeder in Iceland. In N. America main range is from central Alaska n.e. to lake-line MacKenzie – Great Lakes; s.e. to Middle West; s. to lat. 40° N.; w. to Pacific Coast Range;

SHOVELER, duck and drake,
about 1/7 (see also p. 170)

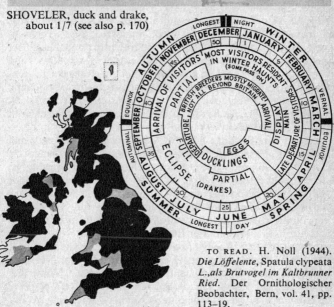

TO READ. H. Noll (1944).
Die Löffelente, Spatula clypeata
L.,*als Brutvogel im Kaltbrunner
Ried.* Der Ornithologischer
Beobachter, Bern, vol. 41, pp.
113–19.

many scattered records beyond. Old World birds winter a short
distance beyond equator; New World birds Caribbean, Hawaii.

MOVEMENTS. British breeders mostly leave us for winter; giving place to invasion of Continental shovelers, arriving on east
coast from Europe and Russia, and passing s. and w. along
usual routes, some to Ireland; back by same routes.

POCHARD *Aythya ferina* (LINNAEUS, 1758)

Very close relation known as REDHEAD in North America.

RECOGNITION. Medium. Length about 18 in., of which body about two-thirds. Weight drake 26–44 oz., duck 27–36 oz. Both sexes have no white on wing and a light blue 'bridge' over middle of black bill, larger in drake. Drake has head rich chestnut; breast black; back and flanks light grey; under-parts white; rump and under-tail black; legs dull grey. Duck is almost wholly dull rippled brown, somewhat lighter (but *not* whitish) on under-parts and whitish on face and throat, especially base bill; legs greenish-grey. Drake in eclipse like grey-backed duck; young like duck. Gait and flight as other diving ducks (see 18a, p. 18); flight fast with whispering sound. Feeds usually in flocks, often hundreds, by diving in shallows; can stay under ½ min.; eats mainly plants (and their seeds), including water-milfoil, bur-marigold, smartweed (*Polygonum*), hornwort, duckweed, pondweed, rush, *Panicum*-grass, *Glyceria*-grass, reed, stonewort and corn; and small fish, amphibians and their tadpoles, insects, crustaceans, molluscs and worms. Voice rare outside breeding-season, of drake cough 'cch-huck' and soft cooing whistle; of duck coarse churr (*not* quack).

BREEDING. Individual. Display on water, drakes round duck dip, stretch and raise head and expand neck; throw head right back to touch back. Nest usually at edge water, often in dense reeds and semi-floating; built by duck with grass and reeds and lined down. Eggs 5–18, normally about 9, laid daily, length 2¼ to 2½ in., dull stone-green. Duck alone incubates, starting on full clutch, for 3½ to 4 weeks; young fly after 7 or 8 weeks; duck deserts young before they can fly. Drakes take no part and flock in clubs. Duckling rather like mallard's, brown with yellow-green face, under-parts and markings. Young usually attains adult plumage in first season after that in which it is hatched.

DISTRIBUTION. Reedy but open fresh waters of the temperate Old World, breeding n. to Orkney, Denmark (not Norway), Sweden to Arctic Circle, Finland to 63° N., Russia to White Sea, R. Dvina, head-basins of R. Volga, Siberia to about 60° N.; e. to L. Baikal; s. to N.W. Mongolia – Altai – Turkestan – Aral – Caspian – Caucasus – Black Sea – Rumania – Yugoslavia – Austria – Germany – Belgium – England; w. to E. England, Anglesey, Lowlands and E. Highlands; with outpost breeding-groups, some erratic, in Ireland, W. England, Wales, W. Highlands and Islands, ? Siberia to mid-Lena and Kamchatka, ? Tunis, Algeria (L. Fezzara), S. Spain, France (Lyon). Winters s. in Europe to

POCHARD, drake and duck, about 1/7 (see also p. 172)

Note: breeding sporadic in many areas.

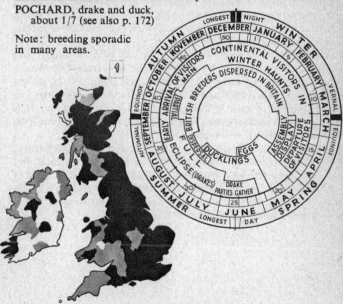

Mediterranean and in Asia not further than Tropic of Cancer.

MOVEMENTS. British breeders disperse to bigger lakes in Britain in winter, flocks being augmented by invasion of Baltic breeders, arriving on east coast and filtering round, through, but not beyond British Isles, including Ireland.

TO READ. E. O. Höhn (1943). *Some observations on the common pochard.* British Birds, vol. 37, pp. 102–07.

FERRUGINOUS DUCK or WHITE-EYE

Aythya nyroca (GÜLDENSTÄDT, 1770)

RECOGNITION. Small-medium. Length about 16 in., of which body about two-thirds. Weight 21–25 oz. Sexes (and young) much alike, though drake has white eye, and duck is duller. Upperparts and head and upper breast chestnut; lower breast and upper belly white; rest of belly grey; under-tail white (good field-character). In flight a curved white band across middle of trailing edge of wing is very noticeable. Bill and legs black. Not very much change in eclipse. Flies much as pochard, feeds usually in pairs and family parties by diving in shallows; can stay under $\frac{3}{4}$ min. (usually under $\frac{1}{2}$ min.); eats mainly plants (and their seeds), including white water-lily, smartweed (*Polygonum*), duckweed, pondweed and sedges; and small fish, amphibians, insects, crustaceans, molluscs and worms. Voice rare outside breeding-season, rather like pochard's.

DISTRIBUTION AND MOVEMENTS. A bird of reedy and 'closed' fresh waters and swamps of the temperate Old World, breeding north to Germany, Poland and about 55° N. across Europe and Asia; east to the R. Yenesei and the Altai Mts., or to Maritime Province USSR if Baer's pochard (*A. n. baeri*) is considered as same species; south to about 35° N. and Himalayas in Asia, Syria (L. Antioch), the Mediterranean, Algeria and Morocco; west to Spain, eastern France, and central Germany; with outposts or occasional breeders in Belgium, Holland and ? Kamchatka (Baer's). Migrates in winter as far as Tropic of Cancer in Asia, in Africa beyond it up the Nile and to Nigeria. Has been seen or shot in Britain over 150 but probably under 200 times, about half of them in East Anglia.

FERRUGINOUS DUCK, drake and duck. about 1/6

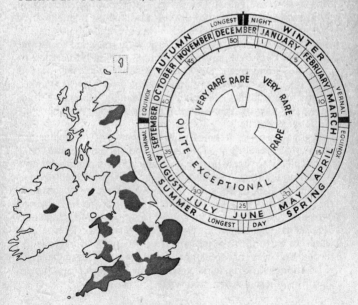

TUFTED DUCK   *Aythya fuligula* (Linnaeus, 1758)

Close relation known as RING-NECKED DUCK in N. America.

RECOGNITION. Medium. Length about 17 in., of which body about two-thirds. Weight drake 23–39 oz., duck 22–33 oz. Both sexes have blue-grey bill and legs: broad white wing-bar extending across almost whole of trailing half of wing; dark under-tail. Drake has head, breast and upper-parts black, with tuft hanging from back of head; belly and flanks white. Duck is almost uniformly dark brown in summer; has white belly in winter; *small* amount of (or no) white at base of bill; under-tail dark brown (compare duck scaup); and detectable tuft (smaller than drake's). Eclipse drakes and male young like ducks but darker. Flies and behaves as other diving ducks. Feeds usually in flocks, not often of more than 100 birds, by diving in shallows; can stay under ¾ min. eats in Britain mainly animals, including fish and amphibians and their spawn and young; many aquatic molluscs, and insects; also dock, smartweed (*Polygonum*), duckweed, pondweed, grasses and berries. Voice rare outside breeding season, of drake a whistle 'hoia', of duck a coarse churr.

BREEDING. Individual. Display on water, bowing, and raising and throwing back of head by drakes; also pursuit-flights of duck by drakes. Nest usually at edge water, in cover though not usually in reeds, often on islets; built by duck with grass and reeds and lined down. Eggs 6–18, normally about 9, laid daily; length 2 to 2½ in., dull stone-green. Duck alone incubates, starting on full clutch, for 3½ to 4 weeks; young fly after 6 or 7 weeks. Drakes take no part and flock in clubs. Brown-and-yellow duckling, rather dark. Young attains adult plumage in first year after that in which it is hatched.

DISTRIBUTION. All kinds of fresh waters of the temperate Old World, breeding n. to Iceland, and in Europe and Asia approximately to forest-line; e. to Kamchatka, Commander and Kurile Islands and north island of Japan; s. to Maritime Province USSR, in E. Asia to about 45° N., in S.W. Asia to Turkestan – Aral – Caspian – Caucasus – Black Sea, in Europe to Bulgaria, Yugoslavia, Austria, Germany, N. France, Holland, England; w. to Ireland, Scotland (not Orkney and Shetland), Faeroe and Iceland. In parts of this range rare breeder (e.g. Austria, Holland, Faeroe), and rare or occasional in isolated places outside it, e.g. L. Antioch in Syria, and Cyprus. Some migrants almost reach equator in winter in Africa and Asia.

TUFTED DUCK, drake and duck, about 1/0 (see also p. 173)

Note: breeding sporadic in many areas.

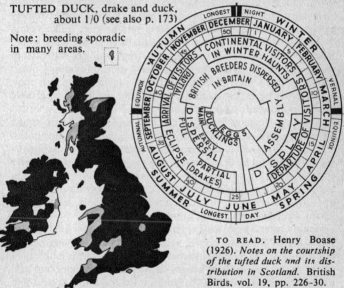

TO READ. Henry Boase (1926). *Notes on the courtship of the tufted duck and its distribution in Scotland.* British Birds, vol. 19, pp. 226-30.

MOVEMENTS. British breeders disperse to bigger lakes in Britain in winter, flocks being augmented by invasion of birds breeding in Iceland and Europe, arriving N. Scotland and E. coast, and passing s. or w. to all suitable waters in, but probably not beyond, British Isles, including Ireland, most individuals probably returning same way, though some may join flocks using different routes.

SCAUP *Aythya marila* (LINNAEUS, 1761)

GREATER SCAUP in North America.

RECOGNITION. Medium. Length about 19 in , of which body about two-thirds. Weight drake 21–48 oz., av. 33 oz., duck 21–47 oz., av. 32 oz. Both sexes have blue-grey bill and legs; bill substantially wider and more spatulate than tufted's; broad white wing-bar extending across almost whole of trailing half of wing; dark under-tail (as tufted duck). Drake has head black glossed with green, no tuft; breast, rump and under-tail black; belly and flanks white; back pale grey, finely pencilled black (compare tufted). Adult duck like tufted but retains white on belly in summer (brown only at edges) and at all times has broad conspicuous white band round base of bill; in summer usually also whitish cheek-spot; under-tail black. Immature ducks may not have white faces, or no more white than tufted, and are extremely hard to distinguish. Drake in eclipse retains grey back; young drakes like dull adult drakes. Feeds usually in large flocks, sometimes over a thousand, by diving in fresh and sea-water from shallows to 3 fathoms; can stay under 1 min., normally $\frac{1}{2}$ min.; probably eats a little more animal than vegetable; mainly molluscs; and insects, crustaceans, worms and small fish; vegetable mainly pondweed; also water-milfoil, musk-grass (N. America) and others. Voice rare away from breeding-place, where drake has cough, whistle, and duck coarse churr, various softer notes.

BREEDING. Individual or social. Display a bowing and throwing-back of head by drake, not beyond vertical. Nest usually near edge of water, not necessarily in cover, often on islet in freshwater or sea-loch, hollowed by duck and lined grass or heather, and down. Eggs 5–13, normally about 9, laid daily, length $2\frac{1}{4}$ to $2\frac{3}{4}$ in., dull greenish. Duck alone incubates, for $3\frac{1}{2}$ to 4 weeks; young fly after 5 or 6 weeks. Drakes guard territory and brood. Duckling olive-brown above, yellow-buff below. Young attains adult plumage in second summer after that in which hatched.

DISTRIBUTION. Open waters of N. temperate moorland and arctic tundra. Breeds in Old World n. to Iceland, Lapland and arctic coast of N. Russia and Siberia; e. to an unknown distance in Siberia; s. to 60° N. in Siberia and Russia (c. 57° N. in W. Russia), Finland, Baltic Islands, Sweden, Norway to c. 63° N., and Faeroe; w. to Faeroe and Iceland; with irregular outpost breeders on ? Bornholm (Denmark), and in Orkney (not Shetland), N. Highlands and Outer Hebrides (1944). In N. Pacific breeds Kamchatka, Commander Is., N. Kuriles. In New World

SCAUP, duck and drake, about 1/0 (see also p. 172)

TO READ. Philip E. Brown (1945). *Observations on a scaup-duck and brood on the Lincolnshire coast.* British Birds, vol. 38, pp. 192–93.

breeds w. to Aleutian Is.; n. to arctic coast w. of Anderson R., Gt. Bear and Gt. Slave Ls.; e. to N. Saskatchewan; s. to 58° N. and coastal mts. Alaska; with outposts beyond. Winters on coasts; in Europe to France, E. Mediterranean and Black Sea; and to Persian Gulf, Japan, California and Caribbean.

MOVEMENTS. To Britain scaup chiefly winter-visitor from Iceland; invasion N. coast and through islands, then along W. coasts and many to Ireland; but also along E. coast; birds reach nearly all shores and some inland waters; not beyond Britain.

129

GOLDENEYE *Bucephala clangula* (LINNAEUS, 1758)
AMERICAN GOLDEN-EYE in North America.

RECOGNITION. Medium. Length drake about 19 in., duck
about 17 in., of which body about 2/3 (neck looks short). Weight
drake 25–46 oz., av. 34 oz., duck 17–36 oz., av. 27 oz. Both sexes
have short bill, head of angular, not rounded outline; back, rump
and wings black, with broad white patch extending over most of
inner half of wing, nearly to leading edge; under-parts and under-
tail white; legs orange. Drake has bill wholly dark; head black
with green and purple gloss, and a round white patch between bill
and eye; neck and breast white, conspicuous. Duck has yellow
tip to dark bill; chocolate-brown head; white collar (adults only);
grey bar across breast and grey flanks. Drake in eclipse, and
immature birds, like duck. Flies swiftly, wing-beats rapid, with
vibrant singing whistling; does not patter on take-off. Feeds in
families, sometimes flocks 100 or more, by diving from shallows
to 3 fathoms; can stay under one min., normally ½ min; eats about
3/4 animal and 1/4 vegetable, crustaceans, insects, molluscs; also
small fish, amphibians and worms; pondweed and sea-weed.
Voice rare away from breeding-place; drake has whistle and
sneeze 'zzee-at', duck usual coarse churr and a definite 'quack'.

BREEDING. Individual. Display of male on water includes
bowing, rearing up, neck-stretching, throwing head back to touch
rump, with kick which throws up little jet of water, and rolling.
Nest usually near water in a hole in a tree (up to 60 ft. above
ground), lined by duck with down. Eggs 5–19, normally about 9,
laid daily, length 2 to 2¾ in., turquoise. Duck alone incubates for
3 to 4½ weeks; ducklings jump from nest when about two days
old, are led to water, fly after 7 to 7½ weeks. Drakes take no part
and flock in clubs. Duckling has upper-parts dark brown, three
pairs white back-patches and white wing-bar; under-parts mostly
white; legs *yellowish*. Young attains adult plumage in second
season after that in which it is hatched.

DISTRIBUTION AND MOVEMENTS. Waters among the great
northern conifer forests of Old and New Worlds in the breeding-
season, and of rivers and coasts in winter. In Old World *B. c.
clangula* breeds n. to forest-line; e. to Bering Straits, Kamchatka
and Sakhalin; s. to about 46° N. across Asia, Russia in Europe
(not Ukraine), N. Poland, N. Germany; w. to R. Elbe, Sweden,
and Norway n. of 61° N.; with outposts near mouth Danube
and in Montenegro; breeding suspected Scottish Highlands,
Denmark and Iceland, and bred Cheshire in 1931 and 1932. In N.
America *B. c. americana* breeds not beyond forest-line in Alaska,

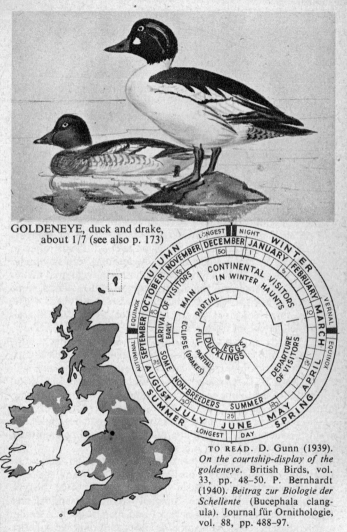

GOLDENEYE, duck and drake, about 1/7 (see also p. 173)

CONTINENTAL VISITORS IN WINTER HAUNTS

MAIN ECLIPSE (DRAKES)

PARTIAL

FULL PARTIAL

EGGS DUCKLINGS

ARRIVAL OF VISITORS

DEPARTURE OF VISITORS

EARLY

SOME NON-BREEDERS

SUMMER

WINTER

AUTUMN

SPRING

SUMMER

LONGEST NIGHT

LONGEST DAY

AUTUMNAL EQUINOX

VERNAL EQUINOX

AUGUST JULY JUNE MAY APRIL MARCH FEBRUARY JANUARY DECEMBER NOVEMBER OCTOBER SEPTEMBER

TO READ. D. Gunn (1939). *On the courtship-display of the goldeneye.* British Birds, vol. 33, pp. 48–50. P. Bernhardt (1940). *Beitrag zur Biologie der Schellente* (Bucephala clangula). Journal für Ornithologie, vol. 88, pp. 488–97.

Canada, Newfoundland and N.E. United States. Winters in Asia s. to T. of Cancer, in Europe Mediterranean; in America S. United States. Many visit coasts and lakes Britain in autumn; most winter though some pass on to S.E. Europe.

LONG-TAILED DUCK

Clangula hyemalis (LINNAEUS, 1758)

OLD-SQUAW in North America.

RECOGNITION. Medium. Length drake with tail-feathers about 21 in., 16 or 17 in. without; duck about 16 in. Body about 2/3 length without tail-feathers. Weight drake 18–37 oz., av. 29 oz., duck 16–31 oz., av. 23 oz. Head small, usually whitish, with steep forehead and short bill; no white on wings; under-parts and flanks white; sharp pointed tail. Drake is dark brown and white; bill pink or orange with black base and tip; in winter is white save for grey face, and dark brown neck-patch, breast-band, mid-line of back, and wings; in summer white is replaced by brown except on belly and under-tail, and sometimes back of head; this is probably early and prolonged 'eclipse' in which bird breeds. Duck has blackish bill; head white with brown on top and some on sides; back brown; under-parts white with brown chest-band; tail pointed but much shorter than drake's. Flies in swinging style, low and fast. Does not patter on take-off. Feeds, often in large flocks, by diving to depths up to 9 fathoms; can stay under $1\frac{1}{2}$ min., normally $\frac{1}{2}$ to $\frac{3}{4}$ min.; eats almost wholly animal matter (90% vol. N. America), mainly crustaceans and molluscs, some insects, fish, worms; vegetable includes grasses, pondweeds, algae, mosses, corn. Voice of drake unforgettable musical 'loudl-oudl-ow', 'a-aadelow', of duck a quack.

BREEDING. Individual. In display drakes crowd a duck, bow, raise heads and tail, arch head back to touch back. Pursuit-flights. Nest a scrape in cover usually near water-edge, lined by duck with down. Eggs 5–11, normally 6 or 7, laid daily, length 2 to $2\frac{1}{4}$ in., olive-buff. Duck alone incubates for about $3\frac{1}{2}$ weeks; ducklings can fly after about 5 weeks. Drakes guard territory until eggs hatch. Duckling dark brown, with small white patches round eye, whitish under-parts. Young attains fully adult plumage in third season after that in which it is hatched.

DISTRIBUTION AND MOVEMENTS. Arctic and sub-arctic lakes and coasts, breeding on the shores of lakes and sheltered seas all round the Polar Basin s. to Norway (n. of 60° N.), N. Sweden, Finland, White Sea, Siberian rivermouths and islands. Pacific coasts as far as Kamchatka and Commander, Aleutian and Kodiak Is., coast, river-mouths and islands of arctic America from Alaska to Labrador (not Hudson's Bay), Greenland, Iceland; with irregular outposts in ? North Kuriles and Faeroe, Orkney and possibly Shetland. In winter feeds offshore round

LONG-TAILED DUCK, drake and duck, about 1/6 (see also p. 175)

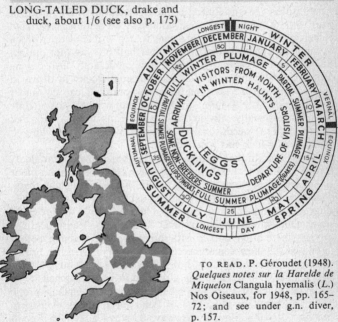

LONGEST NIGHT WINTER JANUARY FEBRUARY
AUTUMN NOVEMBER DECEMBER
OCTOBER FULL WINTER PLUMAGE
SEPTEMBER ARRIVAL VISITORS FROM NORTH PARTIAL SUMMER PLUMAGE
EQUINOX IN WINTER HAUNTS VERNAL EQUINOX
AUTUMNAL EQUINOX MARCH
SUMMER PLUMAGE (FULL) PARTIAL SUMMER PLUMAGE
SOME NON-BREEDERS SUMMER EGGS DUCKLINGS DEPARTURE OF VISITORS (DRAKES)
AUGUST PLUMAGE (ECLIPSE) MOULT FULL SUMMER PLUMAGE APRIL
JULY SPRING
SUMMER JUNE MAY
LONGEST DAY

TO READ. P. Géroudet (1948). *Quelques notes sur la Harelde de Miquelon* Clangula hyemalis (*L.*) Nos Oiseaux, for 1948, pp. 165–72; and see under g.n. diver, p. 157.

British coasts and Channel, in North, Baltic, Black, Caspian and Aral Seas, probably L. Balkash, L. Baikal, in Pacific to Sea of Japan and California, in Great Lakes, along Atlantic coast N. America as far as N. Carolina, and off S. Greenland. Visitors to Britain do not pass beyond; most stay in Shetland, Orkney and Hebrides, quite a number winter along east coast, and a regular few reach Donegal and Mayo. Elsewhere irregular, and rare inland.

EIDER *Somateria mollissima* (Linnaeus, 1758)

RECOGNITION. Medium-large. Length about 2 ft., of which body 3/4. Weight 2¾–6 lbs., av. 4 lbs. (Pacific race to 6½ lbs.) Bulky. Largest British duck. Head large (neck short); flat line of forehead continued along beak. Drake has bill blue-grey and green, head white, with black crown and green nape; breast slightly pink; under-parts and flanks black; back white; rump black with white patch on sides; wing black with whole fore-wing white; legs olive-yellow to green. Duck reddish-brown noticeably barred rather than spotted with black, with two obscure light wing-bars; bill and legs greenish-dusky. Drake in eclipse or juvenile plumage is confusing as mainly blackish, with light streak from bill to, and round, eye; adult can be distinguished from velvet-scoter as has white fore-wing (patch visible at rest) which in flight occupies leading half of inner half of wing (not present on young). Flies usually in files, low, moderately fast, patters to take off calm water. Feeds usually in small flocks, by diving in sea to depths up to 8 fathoms, normally not over 3, can stay under ¾ min., normally ½ min., using feet and wings; eats mainly molluscs, especially mussels; also crustaceans, echinoderms and insects; and sea-weed, sometimes berries. Voice of drake 'ah-oo', 'ah-hee-*oo*'. Duck has harsh churr.

BREEDING. Individual and social. Drakes display round duck, throwing heads vertically upwards. Nest usually scrape on moor or tundra, often some distance inland, in open or slight cover, concealed by cryptic pattern of sitting duck, lined grass and down. Eggs 3–9, normally 4 or 5, laid daily, length 2¾ to 3½ in., greenish-stone. Duck alone incubates for 3½ to 4½ weeks; leads ducklings to sea, where often pooled with other broods; fledging period unknown. Drakes sometimes guard territory. Duckling brown with whitish belly and chin, buff streak over eye. Young attains adult plumage in third season after that in which hatched.

DISTRIBUTION AND MOVEMENTS. A north-temperate-arctic sea duck, breeding round 2/3 of Polar Basin. *S. m. mollissima* breeds n. to Jan Mayen, Norway, S. Novaya Zemlya; e. to Waigatz; s. to coastal tundra Siberia-in-Europe, White Sea, S. Baltic Islands, N. Germany, Denmark, Frisian Is., N. England, and N. Ireland; w. to Iceland and S.E. Greenland with outpost in Brittany; *S. m. borealis* (northern e.) breeds in Franz Josef Land, Spitsbergen, W. Greenland, Ellesmere, Devon and Baffin Islands, Melville Peninsula, Southampton Island and Ungava Bay. *S. m. dresseri* (American e.) breeds from S. Labrador to

134

EIDER, drake and duck,
about 1/9 (see also p. 175)

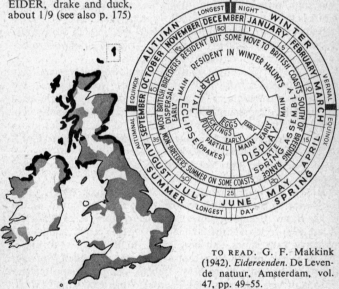

TO READ. G. F. Makkink
(1942). *Eidereenden*. De Leven-
de natuur, Amsterdam, vol.
47, pp. 49–55.

Maine and in Hudson's Bay. *S. m. v-nigrum* (Pacific e.) breeds
in Aleutian Is., Alaska, and on both sides of Bering Strait from
Tchaun Bay to Victoria I. Does not usually move *far* in winter,
in spite of ice; European birds not usually beyond Bay of Biscay.
In Britain steady increase during last hundred years, before which
bred only in Shetland, Orkney and Hebrides. British breeders do
not move far from breeding-place, though irregular winter-visitors
are known in S. England, Wales and S. Ireland.

SCOTER   *Melanitta nigra* (LINNAEUS, 1758)

AMERICAN SCOTER in North America.

RECOGNITION. Medium. Length about 18 in., of which body 2/3. Weight drake 28–51 oz., av. 40 oz., duck 22–45 oz., av. 35 oz. Drake entirely black, except for yellow patch on bill. Duck brown with blackish bill and brown legs; side of head and upper throat pale browny-white, looks whitish. Tail pointed. No wing-bar. Holds bill well up when swimming. Eclipse not well marked. Flies, usually in oblique lines or V's, low and fast with quick whistling wing-beats; patters to take off calm water. Feeds, outside breeding-season usually in large packs, by diving to depths up to 5 fathoms, normally not over 2; can stay under one min; normally ½ min., using feet and wings; eats mainly molluscs (about 2/3 total food), especially mussels; also crustaceans; and (mostly at breeding-place) fish, insects, worms and water-plants, particularly pondweed. Voice of drake querulous musical 'coor-loo', of duck hoarse churr.

BREEDING. Individual. Drakes 'torpedo-rush' ducks and play follow-my-leader. Also bowing ceremonies. Nest usually scrape on moor near margin of fresh-water loch or calm sea-loch, often on islet, lined moss and down. Eggs 5–10, normally about 6, laid daily, length 2¼ to 2¾ in., buff. Duck alone incubates for about 4 weeks, beginning on full clutch; ducklings can fly after 6 or 7 weeks. Duckling dark-brown above, greyish under-parts; small white spot under eye. Young attains adult plumage in second season after that in which it is hatched.

DISTRIBUTION. A north-temperate arctic duck, purely a sea-bird outside the breeding-season, breeding round most of the Polar Basin. Common scoter *M. n. nigra* breeds n. to the arctic coast of Europe and Siberia, and on Bear I., Novaya Zemlya and Waigatz (sometimes Spitsbergen); e. to R. Lena, s. to about 58° N. in European Russia, central Finland and Sweden, Norway, North Highlands; w. to N.W. Ireland (one place) and Iceland (probably *not* Hebrides and Faeroe). American scoter, *M. n. americana*, breeds w. to Kamchatka and R. Kolyma; n. to arctic mainland coast, e. to Anderson River; s. (mostly coastal) to Kodiak Island and Aleutians; with outposts or erratic breeders as far as Ungava Bay, Newfoundland and ? Japan. Common scoter winters mostly in Baltic, North Sea and Atlantic to N.W. Africa (some Mediterranean, Black, Caspian Seas); American scoter mostly in Sea of Japan, on Canadian Pacific coast, and on U.S. Atlantic coast s. to Carolina, some on Great Lakes.

SCOTER, drake and duck,
about 1/8 (see also p. 174)

Note: breeding sporadic
in some areas.

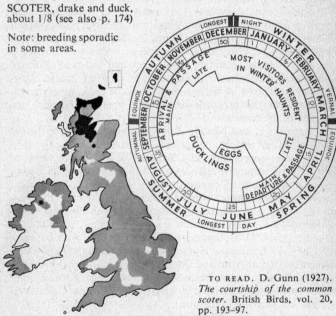

TO READ. D. Gunn (1927).
*The courtship of the common
scoter.* British Birds, vol. 20,
pp. 193–97.

MOVEMENTS. Origin of British winter-birds not clear, though
probably Scandinavian; many birds pass along E. and W. coastal
routes autumn and spring on passage to and from Atlantic coasts
of S.W. Europe and N.W. Africa, and many stay for winter,
particularly in North Sea and Channel coasts and Solway. Winter
quarters of small British breeding population unknown.

VELVET-SCOTER *Melanitta fusca* (LINNAEUS, 1758)

WHITE-WINGED SCOTER in North America.

RECOGNITION. Medium-large. Length about 21 in., of which
body 2/3. Weight drake 2½ to 4½ lbs., av. 3½ lbs., duck 2 to 4 lbs.,
av. 2¾ lbs. Drake black; bill black, smaller knob than common
scoter's, orange-yellow on sides; small white patch behind eye;
legs deep red. Duck dark brown; bill blackish (no knob); on
head two white patches below eye, one in front and one (longer)
behind it; legs dull red. Both sexes have prominent white wing-
patch, occupying trailing half of inner half of wing, usually shows
when bird swimming. Flies heavily but deceptively fast in
formations not usually regular, often low; patters to take off.
Feeds, usually in small flocks, by diving to depths up to 11
fathoms, normally not over 7; can stay under 3 min., normally
not over ¾ min., using feet and wings; eats mainly molluscs (about
3/4 of total food), especially clams, oysters and mussels, which
swallows whole; also crustaceans, insects, worms and fish; and a
few water-plants, including grass-wrack and bur-reed. Voice of
drake a bell-like 'whur-er', repeated; of duck usual hoarse churr.

DISTRIBUTION. A north-temperate arctic duck, purely a sea-
bird outside the breeding-season, but breeding far into the
interior of the continents. Velvet-scoter, *M. f. fusca*, breeds n. to
the arctic coast and Novaya Zemlya (? Spitsbergen); e. to the
R. Yenesei; s. approx. to borders of Russia w. of L. Balkash,
Baltic States and islands, and Sweden; w. to Norway north of
60° N. *M. f. stejnegeri* replaces it in rest of Siberia e. to Bering
Sea, Kamchatka and Commander Is. In W. Alaska is *M. f. dixoni*.
In N. America is white-winged scoter, *M. f. deglandi*, breeding
w. to Yukon and western mountains; n. to arctic coast; e. to
Anderson R., MacKenzie and lake-chain from Great Bear to
Winnipeg; s. to U.S. border and North Dakota; with outposts
and irregular breeders in Hudson's Bay (James Bay), Ungava Bay
(Akpatok I.), Labrador and Quebec. *M. f. fusca* normally winters
as far as Portugal coast, Black Sea and inland seas of Asia; some-
times to Mediterranean; *stejnegeri* to Sea of Japan; *dixoni* to
California, *deglandi* to Carolina.

MOVEMENTS. Origin of British visitors not clear, though probably Scandinavian; summer, winter and on passage, and may
have bred West Ross and Orkney, though not proved. Pass
along coasts, some on way to S.W. Europe, particularly e. and
s. coasts, and winters in certain favourite spots, e.g. Scapa Flow,
Tay, Forth; not common on west.

VELVET-SCOTER, duck and drake, about 1/8 (see also p. 174)

GOOSANDER *Mergus merganser* LINNAEUS, 1758

AMERICAN MERGANSER in North America.

RECOGNITION. Large. Length drake about 26 in., duck about 23 in., of which body about 2/3. Weight drake 2½–4 lbs., av. 3½ lbs., duck 1¾–3 lbs., av. 2½ lbs. Saw-billed. Drake pied; head dark green, no crest; bill and legs red; back black; breast, flanks and under-parts white washed with pink; grey rump and tail; inner wing has leading edge grey, behind which almost fully occupied by clear white patch that joins white of sides of back and neck. Duck brown, grey and white; head and neck chestnut with double crest hanging down back of head and white chin and upper-throat; bill and legs dull red, back and sides grey (sharp change from chestnut neck to grey back); breast and under-parts yellow-pink; leading half of inner wing grey, trailing half white. Drake's eclipse like duck but much more white on wing. Flies low and fast, usually along rivers, cigar-outline; patters to take off. Feeds, usually in small flocks, by diving to depths of about 2 fathoms; can stay under nearly 2 min., normally not over ½ min., using feet and wings; eats mainly fish, also crustaceans, insects, worms, amphibians, and some plants. Voice drake high bubbling whistle, duck hoarse 'karr'; both churr in display.

BREEDING. Individual. Drakes raise heads and bills and yawn, and rise up in breast-preening position, and make torpedo-rushes. Duck stretches and expands crest. Nest in hole in tree or ground, near water, lined down. Eggs 6–17 (? 19), normally 8 or 9, laid daily, length 2½ to 2¾ in., almost white. Duck alone incubates for 4 to 5 weeks, beginning on full clutch; ducklings jump out of nest when 2–4 days old; can fly in about 5 weeks. Drakes play no part and flock in clubs. Duckling see page 145. Young attains adult plumage in second season after that in which it is hatched.

DISTRIBUTION AND MOVEMENTS. Temperate-arctic forest and scrubland rivers, and open waters in winter, breeding to or beyond forest-line of Old and New Worlds. *M. m. merganser*, goosander, breeds n. to Lapland and arctic coast e. to Yalmal, including Novaya Zemlya, and to about arctic circle through Siberia; e. to Kamchatka, Commander and Kurile Is., s. to confines of Russian Asia w. to Aral Sea, and to about 50–55° N. in Russia w. of this, N. Poland, N. Germany, N. Britain; w. to Iceland; outposts in S.E. Europe. *M.*

Black: probable breeding-range towards end 19th century; grey: areas subsequently colonized.

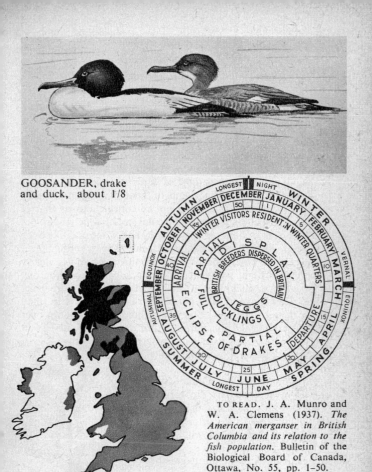

GOOSANDER, drake and duck, about 1/8

TO READ. J. A. Munro and W. A. Clemens (1937). *The American merganser in British Columbia and its relation to the fish population.* Bulletin of the Biological Board of Canada, Ottawa, No. 55, pp. 1–50.

m. orientalis breeds in Central Asia. American merganser, *M. m. americanus*, breeds in Alaska and most of Canada and Newfoundland south to northern U.S. Migrates in Old World not beyond Tropic of Cancer; in New World not often beyond U.S. Unknown as breeder in Britain eighty years ago; breeding-population has increased gradually ever since. British breeders probably resident; in winter influx of birds (? from Scandinavia and Iceland), most marked on e. coasts and in S.E. England; many spend winter Thames reservoirs.

RED-BREASTED MERGANSER

Mergus serrator LINNAEUS, 1758

RECOGNITION. Medium-large. Length drake about 23 in., duck about 21 in., of which body about 3/5. Weight drake 2–3 lbs., av. 2½ lbs., duck 1½–2½ lbs., av. 1¾ lbs. Saw-billed. Drake pied; head dark green, with crest in two bits, top half held horizontal, bottom half hanging down; bills and legs red; back and rump finely pencilled black and white, looks grey; tail grey-brown spotted white; white collar separates head from chestnut breast; under-parts white, flanks grey; fore-wing black, behind which broad white patch occupies most of inner half wing and extends some way onto sides of back and in front of wing; this patch crossed by two black bands and not so conspicuous as that of goosander. Duck has nearly horizontal crest, which does not hang down back of head; is brown, grey and white and like duck (under-parts white), but chestnut of head shades gradually on neck into grey of body, and whitish chin-throat patch not clear y contrasting; in flight wing-patch has black band nearly across, not marked on g. duck. Drake's eclipse like duck but more white on wing. Flies low and fast; patters to take off. Feeds in small flocks by diving to depths of up to 3 fathoms, normally not over 2; can stay under 2 min., normally not over ½ min., using feet and wings; eats mainly fish; also crustaceans, insects, worms and molluscs; not plants. Voice like g's with churring in display.

BREEDING. Individual. Drakes churr, raise heads and yawn, bow, dart, dip, torpedo-rush, bob and wag tails. Nest in close cover on ground, near lake, river or sheltered sea-loch, lined grass and down. Eggs 7–16 (? 19), normally about 9, laid daily, length 2½ to 2¾ in., faintly green-buff. Duck alone incubates for 3½ to 4 weeks, beginning on full clutch. Drakes play no part. Fledging period of duckling (see p. 145) unknown. Young attains adult plumage in second season after that in which it is hatched.

DISTRIBUTION AND MOVEMENTS. North-temperate-arctic rivers and sheltered seas, breeding n. in the Old World to Iceland, Lapland, Novaya

Black: breeding-range before 1837; dark grey: colonized 1837-65; medium grey: 1866-94; light grey: 1895 and after.

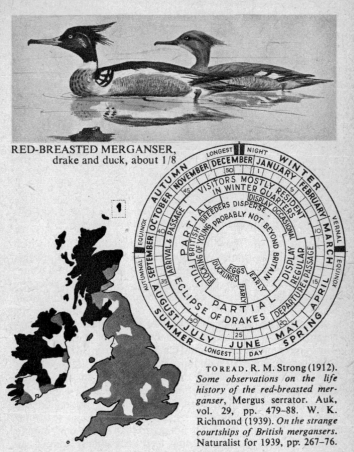

RED-BREASTED MERGANSER,
drake and duck, about 1/8

Diagram text (inner to outer rings):
WINTER · FEBRUARY · JANUARY · DECEMBER · NOVEMBER · OCTOBER · SEPTEMBER · AUTUMN
VERNAL EQUINOX · MARCH · APRIL · SPRING · MAY · JUNE · JULY · AUGUST · SUMMER
AUTUMNAL EQUINOX · ARRIVAL & PASSAGE · DEPARTURE & PASSAGE

LONGEST NIGHT
VISITORS MOSTLY RESIDENT IN WINTER QUARTERS
BRITISH BREEDERS DISPERSE
FLOCKING OF YOUNG PROBABLY NOT BEYOND BRITAIN
PARTIAL · FULL · PARTIAL
DISPLAY OCCASIONAL
DISPLAY REGULAR
ECLIPSE OF DRAKES
EGGS EARLY · DUCKLINGS EARLY
LONGEST DAY

TO READ. R. M. Strong (1912).
*Some observations on the life
history of the red-breasted merganser, Mergus serrator.* Auk,
vol. 29, pp. 479–88. W. K.
Richmond (1939). *On the strange
courtships of British mergansers.*
Naturalist for 1939, pp. 267–76.

Zemlya and arctic rivers of Russia and Siberia; s. to Ireland,
Scotland, Holland, N. Germany, Poland, *c.* 58° in European
Russia, in Asia 50° N. and borders of Russia, Sakhalin, N. Kuriles,
Kamchatka, Commander Is. (outposts Black Sea): in New World
Alaska, Canadian mainland, Great Lakes and Maine region U.S.,
Newfoundland, S.E. Baffin I. and S Greenland. Migrates to N.W.
Africa and Mediterranean, in Asia to T. of Cancer, to Lower Cali-
fornia and Gulf of Mexico. Great increase Britain present century;
no evidence British breeders leave Britain. Iceland birds visit N.
Highlands in winter.

143

SMEW, drake and duck, about 1/6 (see also p. 173)

RECOGNITION. Small-medium. Length about 16 in., of which body about two-thirds. Weight 17 to 26 oz. Smaller than other sawbills with short grey bill; grey legs. Drake is black and white; white with large black patch between eye and bill, black centre of crest, black bands on sides and flanks, grey flanks and tail, black centre to back and black wings, on which prominent white patch occupies most of inner half of leading half. Ducks have chestnut heads, small crest; chin, throat and cheeks contrasting white; grey upper-parts; grey-black wing with slightly smaller white patch than male's on inner half. Immature drake very like duck. Drake in eclipse like duck, more white on wing. Flight extremely, sometimes astonishingly, fast, agile and swinging, can rise easily straight from water. Feeds usually in small flocks (sometimes some hundreds), by diving, in fresh- and sea-water, to unknown depths (probably not great); can stay under $\frac{3}{4}$ minute, normally up to $\frac{1}{2}$ minute, using feet, occasionally wings; eats mainly fish of many kinds; also crustaceans; and amphibians, insects, molluscs and a small amount of plants. Voice very rare outside breeding-grounds; drake whistles and duck churrs.

DISTRIBUTION AND MOVEMENTS. A bird of the waters of the north-temperate forests, in winter of more open waters and sheltered coasts. Breeds in Lapland and throughout Russia (except for extreme western European Russia, Ukraine and Caucasus) north to the forest-line, east to the Pacific; with outposts (? now) in Rumania (Dobrogea) and N. Bulgaria (Lower Danube). Migrates in Europe to Mediterranean; in Asia as far as latitude

30° N., and to intermediate coasts and seas. A winter visitor to Britain, most commonly to S.E. England, especially to reservoirs not far from London, elsewhere decidedly scarce.

TO READ. J. Wolley (1859). *On the breeding of the smew* (Mergus albellus, *L.*) Ibis, vol. 1, pp. 69–76. E. Christoleit (1927). *Bemerkungen zur Biologie der Säger* (Mergus). Journal für Ornithologie, vol. 75, pp. 385–404. P. A. D. Hollom (1937). *Observations on the courtship and mating of the smew.* British Birds, vol. 31, pp. 106–11.

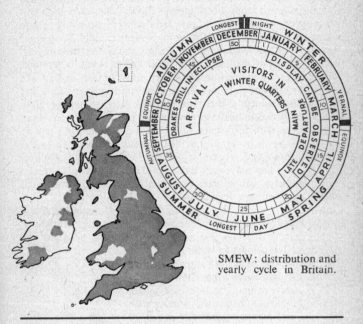

SMEW: distribution and yearly cycle in Britain.

GOOSANDER AND RED-BREASTED MERGANSER DUCKLINGS

The goosander duckling is an obvious sawbill, but hard to tell from red-breasted merganser's; both have dark reddish-brown upper-parts, white lower face, throat and under-parts, two pairs of white back-spots, white wing-patch; and chestnut upper-face. Goosander nestling has nostril at over one-third way from base to tip of bill; red-breasted merganser always under one-third; and goosander nestling has contrasting dark and white streaks under eye.

145

GREAT CRESTED GREBE

Podiceps cristatus (LINNAEUS, 1758)

RECOGNITION. Medium. Length about 18 in., of which body ess than 2/3. Weight 32–41 oz. The largest British grebe. Sexes alike. Long slender neck (front shines very white) held upright, long reddish bill, ear tufts and crest in summer and winter (smaller); back of neck and upper-parts grey-brown; under-parts white; legs green; toes lobed, green-yellow; wings dark with two conspicuous white patches, one (triangular) occupying whole inner half of leading edge of wing, narrowing rapidly along inner edge of wing but not reaching trailing edge, the other (rectangular) occupying part of trailing half of inner half of wing. In summer bill red; crown and crest nearly black; tippet of chestnut on side of head hangs over neck as frill. In winter bill pink, ear-tufts and crest persist (reduced); top of head looks flattened and angular; white line between blackish crown and eye; back greyer than r.n.g's. Flies with fast beats, often high; outline 'cigar'; patters to take off. Feeds in families or loose flocks by diving to over 3 fathoms, normally *c*. $1\frac{1}{2}$; can stay under $\frac{3}{4}$ min., normally not over $\frac{1}{2}$ min.; using feet only; eats mostly insects and fish; also crustaceans, molluscs, amphibians and plants (pondweeds, reed-buds algae); own feathers. Barks, groans, churrs and whickers.

BREEDING. Individual and semi-social. Complex displays mostly on water involving head-shaking, bowing, crouching, diving, rearing out of water, imitation of ghosts, penguins and torpedoes. Nest floats in water-plants near shore, built of reeds by both sexes. Eggs 3–6, normally 4, laid every other day, length $1\frac{3}{4}$ to $2\frac{1}{2}$ in., white at first. Both sexes incubate for about 4 weeks, beginning usually with first egg, and manage young for about 10 weeks, when they can fly. Nestling has pattern of longitudinal black and white stripes on head and upper-parts, white under-parts; bill has two black bands right round. Young attains adult plumage in first season after that in which it is hatched.

Breeding distribution in England in 1860 when only about 42 pairs; none in Wales or Scotland.

DISTRIBUTION AND MOVEMENTS. Fresh waters (and in winter shallow coasts) of temperate–tropical Old World; *P. c. cristatus* breeds n. in Europe and Asia to *c*. 60° N. (66° Finland, N.W. Russia); e. to Pacific; s. to *c*. Tropic of Capricorn; w. to Atlantic (not Iceland).

GREAT CRESTED GREBE, summer plumage, about 1/5 (for winter plumage see p. 177).

The circular diagram contains the following text:

LONGEST NIGHT — WINTER — VERNAL EQUINOX
AUTUMN — AUTUMNAL EQUINOX — SUMMER — LONGEST DAY — SPRING

OCTOBER NOVEMBER DECEMBER JANUARY FEBRUARY MARCH APRIL MAY JUNE JULY AUGUST SEPTEMBER

50 55 1 5 10 15 20 25 30 35 40 45

MAINLY DISPERSED THIS PERIOD — WINTER PLUMAGE — OTHERS STILL ASSEMBLY OF BREEDERS
MAINLY DISPERSED IN WINTER QUARTERS BUT MOVEMENTS NOT UNUSUAL
SECOND BROOD — MAIN — LATE SUMMER INTO WINTER PLUMAGE — MAIN — LATE
EARLY — EARLY
MAIN — FIRST EGGS — MAIN
YOUNG
EARLY
MOULTS INTO WINTER PLUMAGE — DISPERSAL OF BREEDERS
SOME NON-BREEDERS
FULL SUMMER PLUMAGE MOULTS INTO SUMMER

TO READ. Julian S. Huxley (1914). *The courtship habits of the great crested grebe* (Podiceps cristatus). Proc. of the Zool. Soc. London for 1914, pp. 491–562. T. H. Harrisson and P. A. D. Hollom (1932). *The great crested grebe enquiry, 1931.* British Birds, vol. 26, pp. 62–92, 102–3, 142–95.

P. c. infuscatus Africa s. of Sahara; *christiani* Australia; *australis* New Zealand. Reduced by plume-trade, in England, Wales and Scotland to *c*. 42 pairs 1860; but increased with protection to (1931) *c*. 1,240 pairs, since when fairly constant. Grebes of Ireland did not suffer as much. Birds from Baltic migrate to Mediterranean, but those of Britain disperse, not beyond isles, to large lakes, reservoirs and coastal waters.

RED-NECKED GREBE

Podiceps griseigena (BODDAERT, 1783)

HOLBÖLL'S GREBE in North America.

RECOGNITION. Medium. Length about 17 in., of which body about three-fifths. Weight 22–32 oz. Sexes alike. Neck long, not so long or slender as great crested grebe's, held upright, black bill with yellow base; no noticeable crest; no ear-tufts in winter; in winter top of head appears rounded; black crown extends to eye (no white eyestripe); and back is brown (great crested grebe's is grey-brown). At all times dark wing has two white patches like great crested grebe's, but forward patch has rear apex only half-way along inner margin of wing, *not* extending to trailing edge; and under-parts are duller than great crested grebe's. In summer has front and sides of neck chestnut; cheeks pale grey with white border; very distinctive. Flight as great crested grebe; in winter feeds singly (and outside Britain, in loose flocks) by diving, sometimes for nearly a minute, normally for under $\frac{1}{2}$ minute; using feet only; eats mainly fish and amphibians; also crustaceans, insects, molluscs, worms and some plants. Voice rare away from breeding-grounds, where various barks, brayings, and whickerings, and a plaintive loon-cry like great northern diver.

DISTRIBUTION AND MOVEMENTS. A bird of very sheltered, largely forest-, waters (in winter shallow coasts) of temperate-northern Old and New Worlds. In Old World *P. g. griseigena* breeds north in Sweden to 65° N., to E. Lapland, Kola and Archangel; and through nearly all Russia south of the Arctic Circle east to the Ob and its tributaries and Lake Balkash; south in Europe to Bulgaria, Yugoslavia, Austria and Germany; west to Holland (rare) and Denmark (not Norway). *P. g. holböllii* breeds in a wide strip from Lake Baikal; east through E. Asia and N. America to Labrador, including Manchuria, Maritime USSR, N. Japan, Sakhalin, Kamchatka, Asia east of Stanovoi and Anadyr Mts., rivers of western Alaska, Yukon, MacKenzie rivers and lakes (not beyond forest), south Hudson's Bay, Ungava (but not eastern Labrador or Newfoundland), New Brunswick (not Nova Scotia); south through Canada to just over U.S. border from west to east. In Old World species winters as far as Tropic of Cancer; in New World to California and Carolina. Visits Britain in winter (only one record of Holböll's grebe); has been seen nearly all coasts and some inland waters of Lowlands, England and Wales, but only regular east England; extremely rare Ireland.

RED-NECKED GREBE,
summer plumage, about 1/4
(for winter plumage see p. 177).

The circular chart within the image reads:

WINTER · AUTUMN · SUMMER · SPRING

LONGEST NIGHT · DECEMBER JANUARY · FEBRUARY · MARCH · VERNAL EQUINOX · APRIL · MAY · JUNE · LONGEST DAY · JULY · AUGUST · AUTUMNAL EQUINOX · SEPTEMBER · OCTOBER · NOVEMBER

EARLY SPRING MOULT · FULL WINTER PLUMAGE · AUTUMN MOULT · FULL SUMMER PLUMAGE · LATE MOULT · MAIN SPRING MOULT

VISITORS RESIDENT IN WINTER HAUNTS. SOME WEATHER MOVEMENTS · MAIN ARRIVAL OF VISITORS · RARE · LATE DEPARTURE OF VISITORS · MAIN

TO READ. P. O. Swanberg (1929). *Est bo av gråhakedopping* (Podiceps griseigena *Boddaert*) *och några drag ur denna arts biologi.* Fauna och Flora, Uppsala, for 1929, pp. 241–46, L. O. Shelley and F. B. White (1930–31) on *Holboell's grebe in captivity.* Auk, vol. 47, pp. 238–40; vol. 48, pp. 559–63. J. M. Spiers and others (1944). *Holboell's grebe nesting in southern Ontario.* Wilson Bulletin, vol. 56, pp. 206–08.

SLAVONIAN GREBE

Podiceps auritus (LINNAEUS, 1758)

HORNED GREBE in North America

RECOGNITION. Small-medium. Length about 13 in., of which body about 3/5. Weight 11–17 oz. Sexes alike. In winter looks black and white, and noticeably smaller and more short-billed than g.c. or r.-n. grebes; and can only be distinguished from black-necked grebe when close and in good light; has whitish tip to dark bill, which is straight and fairly stout; dark colour of crown does not extend below eye, and white on face and sides of neck almost meets on back of neck; upper-parts blackish, under-parts white. At all times has *one* white patch on wing (no forward triangular patch), on trailing edge, not extending onto outer half of wing. In summer neck, breast and flanks are chestnut, head and tippet black; and prominent group of buff feathers extends from eye back and up as tufts or 'horns'. Flight much as g.c. grebe, feeds singly or in small flocks (large in America) by diving, staying under up to 1 min. (3 alleged), normally ¼ to ½ min. using feet only; eats mainly insects and crustacea; also fish, reptiles, amphibians, molluscs, arachnids, plants; and own feathers. Voice a chattering trill; also croaks, cackles, grunts, croonings and shrieks.

BREEDING. Individual or semi-social. Displays involve rearing out of water, crouching, head-jerking and bowing; male may offer female fish. Nest usually floats among water-plants near shore, built of mud and reeds by both sexes. Eggs 3–10, normally about 4 in Britain, more further north, probably laid every other day, length 1¾ to 2 in., white at first. Both sexes incubate for 3 to 3½ weeks, begin mid- or end-clutch, and manage young ? *c.* 5 weeks. Occasionally second brood. Nestling black and light long-striped, rather darker than g.c.g.'s. Most, but not all, young attain adult plumage in first year after that in which hatched.

DISTRIBUTION AND MOVEMENTS. Quiet northern waters, and in winter sheltered coasts of Europe, Asia and North America; breeding in Old World n. to Iceland, Lapland and in Russia about 65° N.; e. to Sakhalin and R. Amur; s. to about 48° N. in Asia and about 56° N. in Europe, Baltic Islands of Sweden, C. Sweden and Norway, N. Highlands; w. to Faeroe and Iceland; in New World Alaska, Canada (not far beyond forest, and *not* Newfoundland or Newf.–Labrador), and n. edge U.S. Old World birds rarely move s. of 40° N. in summer; New World birds to T. of Cancer. British breeders probably resident, joined (and outnumbered) round coasts autumn and winter by visitors and passengers, ? from Iceland and Scandinavia.

SLAVONIAN GREBE,
summer plumage, about 1/3

Note: breeding irregular
in some areas.

TO READ. On *nesting, etc., in Britain*, A. D. Dubois (1920). British
Birds, vol. 14, pp. 2–10; S. and A. S. Gordon (1928), vol. 22, pp. 2–5;
E. J. Hosking (1939), vol. 33, pp. 170–73. E. Lönnberg (1923). *Några ord
om svarthakedoppingen*, Podiceps auritus *Lin., och dess utbredning i Sverige.*
Fauna och Flora, Uppsala, for 1923, pp. 221–27. B. Olsoni (1928). *Om
svarthakedoppingens* (Podiceps auritus *L.*) *häckning.* Ornis Fennica, Helsing-
fors, vol. 5, pp. 65–72.

BLACK-NECKED GREBE

Podiceps nigricollis Brehm, 1831

EARED GREBE in North America.

RECOGNITION. Small. Length about 12 in., of which body about 3/5. Weight about 10 oz. Sexes alike. General appearance very similar to S.g.; bill dark, whitish tip, more slender than S.g.'s and nearly always tip-tilted. At all times has single white patch on wing, on trailing edge as S.g.'s but extending (not eared grebe) a little way onto outer half of wing. In winter black of crown usually extends below eye and well down over ears; white on cheeks, etc., does not extend towards nape but leaves continuous broad line down back of neck. In summer compares thus with S.g.; somewhat shyer (in Britain), forehead much steeper, crown higher; neck black; tuft of buff-gold feathers extends *back*, not up, fan-wise from eye to form 'ears'; tends to swim with neck curved. Flight as S.g.: feeds singly or in flocks by diving to *c.* 3 fathoms, may stay under over ¾ min., normally *c.* ½ min., using feet only; also snaps up flies; eats mainly insects; also amphibians, crustacea, molluscs; a li tle plant matter; own feathers; fish recorded. Voice 'poo-eep', and 'hicker-whicker'.

BREEDING. Usually social; colonies large in America. Displays involve breast to breast rearing out of water, crouching, head-shaking, torpedo-rushing. Nest usually floating among plants near shore, built of rotten weeds by both sexes. Eggs 2–9, normally 3, ? laid every other day, length 1½ to 2 in., white at first. Both sexes incubate for 3 weeks, beginning on first egg, and manage young for an unknown period. Second brood occasional. Nestling darker than S.g.'s, and stripes more obscure; two black bands on bill extend to both mandibles (only upper on S.g.). Young attains adult plumage in first year after that in which it is hatched.

DISTRIBUTION AND MOVEMENTS. Quiet reedy waters of the W. Old World, W. North America and Africa, and lakes and sheltered coasts in winter. Black-necked grebe, *P. n. nigricollis* (Eurasia) breeds n. to about 58° N.; e. to about 90° E. (Tomsk), Turkestan, Afghanistan and Baluchistan; s. to Persia, Iraq, Palestine, Mediterranean and N.W. Africa; w. to Spain, France and Ireland, *P. n. gurneyi* breeds in nearly all Africa s. of Sahara. *P. n. californicus*, eared grebe, breeds in W. Canada and U.S. B.-n. grebe winters s. to T. of Cancer; e. grebe to C. America. In Britain breeding colonies few and, except one or two, desultory; fairly common (? from W. Europe) in winter and as passenger Cheshire, Midlands, S.E. England; elsewhere irregular.

BLACK-NECKED GREBE, summer plumage, about 1/3 (for winter plumage see p. 177)

Note: breeding sporadic in most areas.

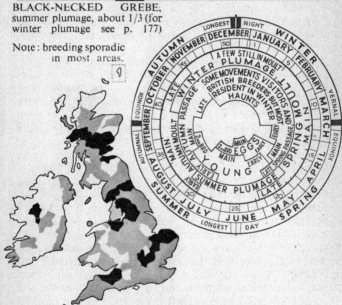

TO READ. O. G. Pike (1919). *The black-necked grebe.* British Birds, vol. 13, pp. 146–54. C. Oldham (1921). *Nesting of the black-necked grebe (Podiceps nigricollis) in Hertfordshire.* Transactions of the Hertfordshire Natural History Society, vol. 17, pp. 211–19. C. G. Connell (1930). *The black-necked grebe. First breeding records for Scotland.* Scottish Naturalist for 1930, pp. 105–09. C. V. Stoney and G. R. Humphreys (1930). *Breeding of the black-necked grebe in Ireland.* British Birds, vol. 24, pp. 170–73 (note by H. F. Witherby, pp. 173–75).

DABCHICK *Podiceps ruficollis* (PALLAS, 1764)

LITTLE GREBE of British List.

RECOGNITION. Small. Length about 10 in., of which body about 3/5. Weight about 5 oz. Sexes alike. The smallest British grebe; neck relatively short; more squat than S. or b.-n. grebe; looks wide and dumpy; white wing-patch on trailing edge of inner half of wing, but much less conspicuous than on other grebes; bill relatively short and stout, black, extreme tip light, yellow-green at base. Winter plumage brown and light, not blackish and white; upper-parts medium-brown, under-parts whitish-brown, cheeks and sides of neck buff. In summer no head ornaments; black and dark brown with cheeks, throat and front of neck chestnut; and yellow-green round gape of jaw becomes lighter and conspicuous. Flies with rapid beats, usually low, patters to take off; feeds singly or in small flocks by diving, staying under up to *c.* ½ min., normally *c.* ¼ min., using feet only; eats fish, molluscs, insects, crustaceans, some plants. Voice, a whistle 'phwit'; in spring a characteristic purring trill.

BREEDING. Individual. Much mutual display, with both sexes trilling, neck-stretching, chasing, offering building material. Nest usually aground in reedy or covered shallows, built of rotten weeds by both sexes. Eggs 3–10; normally about 5, laid every other day, length 1¼ to 1¾ in., white at first. Both sexes incubate for about 3 weeks, beginning on first egg, and manage young for 4–6 weeks, after which they can fly. Double- or even treble-brooded. Nestling striped brown and light, rather like g.c. grebe's, but face 'patched'; bill has one black band near base, not meeting round lower mandible. Young attains adult plumage in first season after that in which it is hatched.

DISTRIBUTION. Nearly all waters of the temperate and tropical Old World and Australasia. Breeds n. to Orkney, S. Sweden and Baltic States and about 52° N. in European Russia, in Asia to Caspian, Aral, Turkestan, Himalayas, China, Korea and Japan; w. to Atlantic; e. to Pacific; s. through Africa, Persia, India, Burma, Malaysia and East Indies to Australia and Tasmania (not N.Z.). Limits of British breeding race *P. r. ruficollis* appear to be on east Urals, N. and W. Caspian, Caucasus, Syria and Palestine (not Egypt), and on south Mediterranean and N.W. Africa. Elements of this subspecies may move s. in winter, often to sheltered coasts, beyond breeding-range to about Tropic of Cancer, including Atlantic Islands.

DABCHICK, summer plumage about 2/7 (for winter plumage see p 176)

MOVEMENTS. British breeders dispersive, often to coasts; no evidence of migration from islands. Winter population swollen by birds (? from N.W. Europe) which invade E. coast; some pass on.

TO READ. Various *notes on the little grebe, display and habits*, in British Birds by J. S. Huxley (1919), vol. 13, pp. 155–58; G. Bird (1933), vol. 27, pp. 34–37; P. H. T. Hartley (1933 and 1937), vol. 27, pp. 82–86; vol. 30, pp. 266–75; and by R. Zimmermann (1928) in the Mitteilungen des Vereins sächsischer Ornithologen, Dresden, vol. 2, pp. 169–74; W. Eltringham (1932) in the Vasculum, Newcastle, vol. 18, pp. 127–30; and G. R. Mountfort (1934) in le Oiseau, Paris, vol. 4, pp. 554–58.

GREAT NORTHERN DIVER

Colymbus immer BRÜNNICH, 1764

(COMMON) LOON in North America.

RECOGNITION. Large. Length about 2 ft. 6 in., of which body about 2/3. Weight 7½–12 (? 15) lbs. The largest British diver. Sexes alike. Bill black, very stout and heavy, evenly tapered. Under-parts white. In winter upper-parts dark, head slightly darker than back, back faintly barred white (adults). In summer head and neck black with purple and green gloss; an incomplete collar and short throat-band formed of vertical white streaks show as light patches; entire upper-parts conspicuously spotted and barred white; under-parts white with black streaks on side of breast. Patters to take off water, for long distance; cannot take off land; flies very fast with fast wing-beats, occasionally glides; cigar-shape, neck dropped a little below 'shoulders'. Feeds in pairs or small flocks, by diving to depths of over 5 fathoms; can stay under 3 min., normally about ¾ min.; uses mainly feet but sometimes wings; eats mostly fish; also crustaceans, worms and molluscs: young birds, reptiles, amphibians, insects and plants recorded. Voice a quack in flight, on water many eerie wails, of pattern 'ah-ooo-oo'; the loon-cry.

BREEDING. Individual. Much mutual courtship, torpedo-chases, and rearing up of body. Display-flights with glides. Nest open, on islet in or by shore of large loch, of rotting plants. Eggs 1–3, normally 2, laid at 2-day interval, length 3¾ to 4 in., olive-brown, a few dark spots. Both sexes incubate 4 or 4½ weeks, beginning first egg, and manage young ? 6 or 7 weeks. Single brood. Nestling dark brown, grey-white under-parts. Young attains adult plumage in second season after that in which it is hatched.

DISTRIBUTION. Large quiet lakes of north-temperate-arctic America in summer, and mainly the sea-coast of the N.E. Pacific, N. Atlantic and North Sea (sometimes Baltic and W. Mediterranean) in winter. Breeds n. to Alaska, MacKenzie, Melville Sound, Barrow Strait, Hudson's Bay, central Baffin I., W. Greenland; e. to Atlantic; s. to about 41° N. in U.S. (40° in California); w. to Pacific, Alaska and Kiska in Aleutian Is.; with extension of breeding range (into Palearctic) along coast E. Greenland, to Iceland (common in parts), Spitsbergen and desultorily to Jan Mayen, Bear Island, ? Faeroe. Unfledged young reported with parents in Shetland, but breeding not proved.

GREAT NORTHERN DIVER, summer plumage, about 1/7 (for winter plumage see p. 176)

MOVEMENTS. To Britain winter-visitor, presumably from Greenland and Iceland, common Highland coasts, and occasional large inland waters. Some non-breeders summer N. Scotland.

TO READ. F. N. Wilson (1927). *The loon at close range.* Bird-Lore, New York, vol. 31, pp. 95–103, O. J. Gromme (1929). *In search of the loon* (Gavia immer) *with movie camera.* Wilson Bulletin, Sioux City, vol. 41, pp. 203–07. J. A. Munro (1945). *Observations of the loon in the Cariboo Parklands, British Columbia.* Auk, vol. 62, pp. 38–49. A. W. Schorger (1947). *The deep diving of the loon and old-squaw and its mechanism.* W.B., vol. 59, pp. 151–59.

BLACK-THROATED DIVER

Colymbus arcticus LINNAEUS, 1758

BLACK-THROATED LOON and PACIFIC LOON in North America.

RECOGNITION. Medium-large. Length about 2 ft., of which body about 2/3. Weight about 7 lbs. Sexes alike. Bill black, evenly tapered, thicker than r.-t.d.'s. Under-parts white. In winter upper-parts uniformly dark (compare g.n.d.); head slightly *lighter* than back. In breeding-season head and back of neck grey; front of neck black; sides of back and feathers over wing (scapulars) show marked area of broad white bands, rest of back black; sides of neck and breast have long vertical black and white streaks. Takes off after pattering (not so slowly as g.n.d.); flies as g.n.d. Feeds in pairs or flocks, by diving to depths of over 3 fathoms; can stay under nearly 2 min., normally not more than ¾ min., uses feet and wings; eats mostly fish; also frogs, crustaceans, worms, molluscs. Voice clucking 'kok, kok' in flight, on water many eerie wails, growls, croaks, barks, groans, screams, howls.

BREEDING. Individual. Display unknown; main courtship at sea before flocks break up. Nest open, on islet in, or shore of large loch, scrape, sometimes lined rotting plants. Eggs 1–3, normally 2, laid at two-day interval, length 3 to 3½ ins., olive-brown with some dark spots. Both sexes (mainly female) incubate 4 to 4½ weeks, beginning first egg, and manage young 8 or 9 weeks. Single brood. Nestling dark brown with lighter under-parts. Young probably attains adult plumage in second season after that in which it is hatched.

DISTRIBUTION AND MOVEMENTS. Largish freshwater lochs throughout the north-temperate-arctic in summer, and N. Pacific, N. Atlantic, Mediterranean, Black, Caspian–Aral sea-coasts in winter. Breeds n. to Polar Basin but not Greenland or islands of Polar Sea except those s. of Lancaster Sound, the Cary Is. in Smith Sound and ? N. Zemlya. In Europe *C. a. arcticus* with s. limit Highlands, Norway, Sweden, E. Baltic, and in Russia lat. 54° or 55° N.; has bred Iceland, Faeroe. In W. Asia *C. a. suschkini* with s. limit N. Caspian – Aral – Balkash. In E. Asia *C. a viridigularis* extends across Bering Straits to W. coast Alaska, breeds s. to Maritime Province USSR, Hokkaido, Kuriles, Kamchatka, Aleutians. In N. America Pacific loon *C. a. pacificus* breeds w. to Alaska Peninsula and Point Barrow; s. to lat. 53° or 54° N. from British Columbia (Q. Charlotte Is.) to Hudson's Bay, and to Southampton I., possibly to Nottingham and Baffin Is. In Britain uncommon outside Highlands, but regular winter-visitor

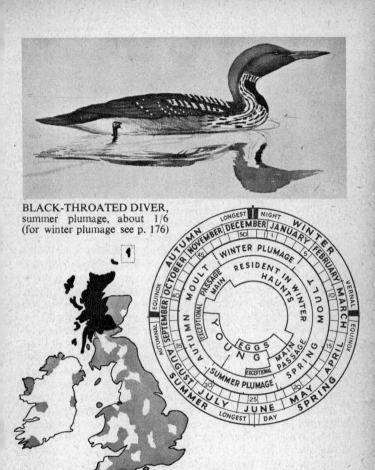

BLACK-THROATED DIVER,
summer plumage, about 1/6
(for winter plumage see p. 176)

to coasts and some inland waters of Scotland (British stock being supplemented then, presumably, from N.W. Europe), and fairly regular E. England. Rare elsewhere.

TO READ. J. M. McWilliam (1931). *On the breeding of the black-throated and red-throated divers in south Argyllshire.* Scottish Naturalist for 1931, pp. 161–64. G. Bodenstein and E. Schüz (1944). *Vom Schleifenzug des Prachttauchers* (Colymbus arcticus). Ornithologische Monatsberichte, vol. 52, pp. 98–105. G. K. Yeates (1945). *The black-throated diver, most handsome of British water birds.* Field, vol. 186, pp. 116–17. Niall Rankin (1947). *Haunts of British divers.* London, Collins, pp. 47–64.

RED-THROATED DIVER

Columbus stellatus PONTOPPIDAN, 1763

RED-THROATED LOON in North America.

RECOGNITION. Medium-large. Length about 2 ft., of which body about two-thirds. Weight about 5 lbs. Sexes alike. The smallest British diver, but not in field noticeably smaller than b.t.d. Bill slender, up-tilted, pale grey. Under-parts white. In winter upper-parts greyer than those of other two divers and speckled with fine white spots; crown and back of neck grey. In summer head and sides of neck ash-grey-brown, back dark grey-brown, uniform dull red throat-patch (looks dark). Usually patters to take off, but may 'jump'; flight fast. Feeds in pairs or flocks, by diving to depths up to 5 fathoms; can stay under $1\frac{1}{2}$ min., but normally under 1 min., uses feet and wings; eats mostly fish; also molluscs, crustaceans, amphibians, insects and plant-matter. Voice in flight a clucking 'kuk-kwuk', on water many eerie wails, growls, hoots, goose-notes, screams and howls.

BREEDING. Individual or semi-social. Display includes 'Plesiosaurus-races', imitations of ghosts rising from water, snake-ceremonies, intruder-scaring, follow-my-leader; and dives and twists in flight. Nest open, on islet in or shores of small tarn, scrape, sometimes lined rotten weeds. Eggs 1–3, normally 2, laid at 2-day interval, length $2\frac{3}{4}$ to $3\frac{1}{4}$ in., olive-brown with some dark markings. Both sexes (mainly female) incubate $3\frac{1}{2}$ to $4\frac{1}{2}$ weeks, beginning first egg; manage young *c.* 8 weeks. Single brood. Nestling indistinguishable from b.t.d.'s. Young attains adult plumage in second season after that in which it is hatched.

DISTRIBUTION. Mountain and tundra tarns of the arctic and sub-arctic in summer, and coasts of N. Pacific, N. Atlantic, N. Sea, Baltic, Mediterranean and Black Seas, inland 'seas' and great lakes of Asia, Persian Gulf, and great lakes of America in winter. Breeds n. round whole Polar Basin and arctic is. (only Jan Mayen doubtful); s. to Donegal, N.W. Highlands and is., Norway, Sweden, Finland, about 55° N. in European and Asiatic Russia, Sakhalin, N. Kuriles, Kamchatka, Commander Is., Kuriles, Alaska, Q. Charlotte Is., Vancouver I., N. British Columbia, Great Slave L., Hudson's Bay to Churchill, Quebec–Labrador Peninsula (not S.W.), Gaspé Pna., New Brunswick, Nova Scotia, Newfoundland, Greenland, Iceland, Faeröe.

MOVEMENTS. British breeders not proved to move beyond British seas; reinforced by birds from other countries in winter

RED-THROATED DIVER,
summer plumage, about 1/6 (for
winter plumage see p. 176)

The diagram (circular calendar) contains the following text:

LONGEST NIGHT — WINTER — LONGEST DAY
WINTER · AUTUMN · SUMMER · SPRING
JANUARY FEBRUARY MARCH APRIL MAY JUNE JULY AUGUST SEPTEMBER OCTOBER NOVEMBER DECEMBER
VERNAL EQUINOX · AUTUMNAL EQUINOX
AUTUMN MOULT LATE · FEW STILL MOULTING
MAIN · WINTER PLUMAGE · EARLY
VISITORS AND BRITISH BREEDERS RESIDENT IN WINTER HAUNTS
ARRIVAL OF VISITORS · DISPERSAL OF BREEDERS
MAIN DEPARTURE OF VISITORS · ASSEMBLY OF BREEDERS
EGGS
YOUNG
EXCEPTIONAL
PLUMAGE · LATE · SPRING MOULT · MAIN · EARLY
35 40 45 50 · 5 10 15 · 20 25 30
EARLY · MAIN

when fairly common all coasts; though rarer S. Ireland. Not rare
inland lakes. Spring passage better marked than autumn.

TO READ. *Notes on habits* in British Birds, by G. J. van Oordt and
J. S. Huxley (1922). *Spitsbergen,* vol. 16, pp. 34–46; N. Gilroy (1923).
Sutherland, vol. 16, pp. 318–21. D. B. Keith (1937). *North-East Land,* vol.
31, pp. 66–81. J. S. Huxley (1923). *Courtship activities in the red-throated
diver* . . . . Journal of the Linnean Society, vol. 35, pp. 253–92. R. A.
and H. S. Johnson (1935). *A study of the nesting and family life of the red-
throated loon.* Wilson Bulletin, vol. 47, pp. 97–103. N. Rankin (1937). See
under b.-t.d., pp. 82–96.

FIELD IDENTIFICATION

The following pictures are introduced to help the observer to distinguish various birds of prey and waterfowl in flight or in winter plumage. The reader's attention must be drawn to the remarks on p. 174 of Vol. I of this series, where some principles of field-noting and identification are set out.

HARRIERS

MARSH-
(IMMATURE MALE)

HEN-
(FEMALE)

MONTAGU'S
(FEMALE)

PEREGRINE

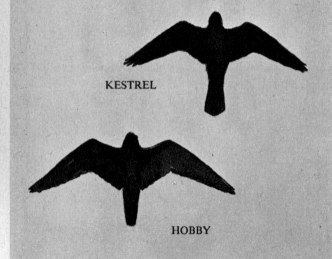

KESTREL

HOBBY

ICELAND
GREENLAND
OR GYR-

MERLIN

SPARROW-HAWK

GOLDEN EAGLE

BUZZARD

ROUGH-LEGGED
BUZZARD

BIRDS OF PREY

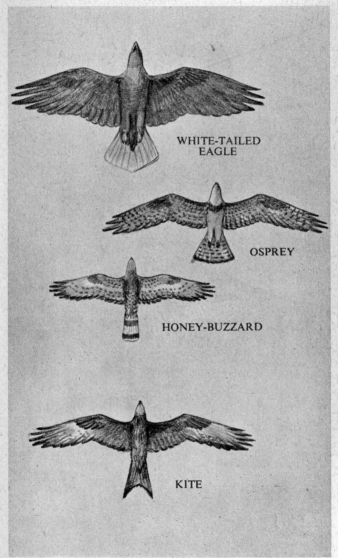

WHITE-TAILED
EAGLE

OSPREY

HONEY-BUZZARD

KITE

SWANS

MUTE

WHOOPER

BEWICK'S

CANADA

BARNACLE-

BRENT

MALLARD

WIGEON

SHOVELER

TEAL

GARGANEY

PINTAIL

GADWALL

POCHARD

SCAUP

11

TUFTED

GOLDENEYE

SMEW

SCOTER

VELVET-SCOTER

LONG-TAILED DUCK
(WINTER)

SURF-SCOTER

EIDER

GREAT NORTHERN D

BLACK-THROATED D

RED-THROATED D

DABCHICK

GREBES IN WINTER

GREAT CRESTED G

RED-NECKED G

BLACK-NECKED G

SLAVONIAN G

EXTREME RARITIES

The following is the list of birds of prey and water-fowl which have been seen or obtained in Britain, but which are so rare that they have not, in my opinion, merited any full mention. Their *Handbook* numbers, and (in brackets) the approximate number of times they have been observed, are given.

Those marked * *may* by now have been seen a hundred times.

W 245	Eagle-owl, *Bubo bubo* (c. 14).	
W 246-7	Hawk-owl, *Surnia ulula* (8).	
W 248	Tengmalm's owl, *Aegolius funereus* (c. 46).	
W 252	Scops-owl, *Otus scops* (c. 62).	
W 264	Lesser kestrel, *Falco naumanni* (14).	
W 265	Red-footed falcon, *Falco vespertinus* (c. 70).	
W 267	Spotted eagle, *Aquila clanga* (c. 14).	
W 274	Pallid harrier, *Circus macrourus* (3).	
W 279	Black kite, *Milvus migrans* (5).	
W 282	Griffon-vulture, *Gyps fulvus* (3).	
W 283	Egyptian vulture, *Neophron percnopterus* (2).	
W 286	Black stork, *Ciconia nigra* (c. 29).	
W 290	Purple heron, *Ardea purpurea* (c. 93).	
W 291	Great white heron (American egret), *Egretta alba* (c. 7).	
W 292	Little egret, *Egretta garzetta* (c. 12).	
W 293	Buff-backed heron, *Ardeola ibis* (2).	
W 294	Squacco heron, *Ardeola ralloides* (c. 91).	
W 298	American bittern, *Botaurus lentiginosus* (c. 47).	
W 299	Flamingo, *Phoenicopterus ruber* (c. 22).	
W 305	Lesser white-front, *Anser erythropus* (c. 12).	
W 308-9	Snow-goose, *Anser hyperboreus* (c. 35).	
W 310	Red-breasted goose, *Branta ruficollis* (9).	
W 316	Ruddy shelduck, *Casarca ferruginea.**	
W 321	Blue-winged teal, *Anas discors* (9).	
W 324	American wigeon (Baldpate), *Anas americana* (11).	
W 327	Red-crested pochard, *Netta rufina* (c. 42).	
W 333	Buffel-headed duck, *Bucephala albeola* (4).	
W 335	Harlequin-duck, *Histrionicus histrionicus* (6).	
W 336	Steller's eider, *Polysticta stelleri* (4).	
W 338	King-eider, *Somateria spectabilis* (c. 50).	
W 341	Surf-scoter, *Melanitta perspicillata* (see opposite).**	
W 345	Hooded merganser, *Mergus cucullatus* (4 or more).	
W 377	White-billed northern diver, *Colymbus adamsii* (4).	

SURF-SCOTER *Melanitta perspicillata* (LINNAEUS, 1758)

SURF-SCOTER, drake and duck, about 1/7 (see also p. 175)

Probably the least rare of these extreme rarities. The ruddy shelduck, though recorded slightly more often, is widely kept in captivity, and some of its records are undoubtedly of escapers; the surf-scoter has never been kept in captivity, and its British records are all genuine. These mostly Orkney and Shetland. A New

World breeder, based mainly on the Great Slave–Great Bear–Mackenzie River region of the Canadian North-West; may occasionally breed in Labrador, Greenland. Winters chiefly Great Lakes and e. and w. U.S. seaboards. Length *c.* 21 in., of which body 2/3. Weight 23-40, av. 34 oz. No white on wing. Head more eider-like than other scoters, of drake, with white patch on forehead and another on back of head and nape of neck, of duck with light patches on side like velvet-scoter. Bill of drake patterned red, yellow, white and black.

INDEX

PLEASE TURN OVER

TO THE SECRETARY
THE ROYAL SOCIETY FOR THE PROTECTION
  OF BIRDS
82 VICTORIA STREET,
LONDON, SW1

Having read James Fisher's *Bird Recognition*, Vol. 2,
I would like to join the Royal Society for the
Protection of Birds, and enclose a subscription
(Fellows of the Society pay a guinea a year or more,
Members 10s., or more, or 5s. if under 21 years).
I am interested in the Society and would like some
literature about it.

Name ....
(MR, MRS, MISS, ETC.)

Address ....

   ....

   .... *Date*............

PLEASE WRITE IN BLOCK CAPITALS AND CROSS
OUT WHAT DOES NOT APPLY

THE ROYAL SOCIETY
FOR THE PROTECTION OF BIRDS

This old-established society (it was founded in 1889 and incorporated under Royal Charter in 1904) was originally started to combat the plumage trade, which involved barbarous cruelties to egrets and other beautiful birds. Now its main efforts are exerted to increase the number and variety of British wild birds; to preserve all that are rare, beautiful or scientifically interesting; to prevent any sort of cruelty to wild birds – deliberate or otherwise; and to influence and educate public opinion about birds.

To these ends it:

Owns or manages many sanctuaries in the British Isles, where birds nest which are in special need of protection, often in surroundings of great beauty;

Supports generally the conservation of wild animals and plants in their natural communities, and particularly the preservation of natural marshland, mountain and moorland, and coastland;

Upholds, and strives to improve, the Wild Birds Protection Acts, under which the taking or killing of most British birds and their eggs is unlawful;

Spreads the knowledge and love of birds among old and young by means of films, lectures, meetings, exhibitions, posters and competitions (in particular by open essay competitions and by a Bird and Tree Festival Scheme for schools);

Organizes, in collaboration with the British Trust for Ornithology (see overleaf) the Junior Bird Recorders' Club for boys and girls between the ages of fourteen and eighteen;

Publishes the quarterly magazine *Bird Notes* (free to Fellows and Members), and many reports and pamphlets.

There is a tear-off form for Fellowship (or Membership) on the opposite page.

Note: The R.S.P.B. and the B.T.O. (overleaf) each have quite different kinds of work to do. They are in no possible sense rivals or competitors; but often collaborate, *e.g.* in the exchange of information.

THE BRITISH TRUST FOR ORNITHOLOGY

This relatively new organization (it was founded in 1933 and incorporated as a Company in 1939) was started for the purpose of increasing our knowledge of British birds, by means of observation and experiment in the field, *i.e.*, out of doors.

To this end it:

Has successfully promoted the establishment of the Edward Grey Institute of Field Ornithology at Oxford, which is already the recognized centre of scientific study of the living bird in Britain;

Organizes and supports enquiries and investigations, some co-operative, some individual: among those already undertaken and reported upon are enquiries on the life-history of swallows, the distribution of woodcock, the food of the little owl, the numbers of the black-headed gull, the spread of the fulmar, the numbers and economic value of rooks and woodpigeons, the distribution of the ' bridled ' form of the common guillemot, the history of the corncrake, the opening of milk bottles by tits, the spread of the black redstart, the migratory movements of swifts, waders and terns, and the nesting population of great crested grebes;

Promotes annual investigations of the nesting of all common birds (the Nest Records Enquiry) and of the numbers of herons;

Administers the national scheme for marking wild birds with numbered rings to provide information about their migrations, longevity and other problems;

Co-ordinates the scientific activities of the several Bird Observatories on the coasts of Britain, established for the study of migration;

Holds many scientific meetings and discussions in different parts of Britain;

Maintains the Alexander Library at Oxford, jointly with the University (a useful range of publications can be borrowed by members through the post);

Gives information and advice to bird-watchers on useful subjects for research and investigation, both from its office and by means of regional representatives all over the British Isles; also considers applications for small grants in aid of research by groups or individuals;

Publishes frequent *Bulletins*, annual *Reports*, occasional field guides, and circulates a summary of *Recent Publications in Bird Biology*.

There is a tear-off form for Membership on the opposite page.

To Hon. Secretary
The British Trust for Ornithology
2 King Edward Street,
Oxford

Having read James Fisher's *Bird Recognition*, Vol. 2, I would like to join the British Trust for Ornithology, and enclose a subscription (the Trust asks its members to pay £1 a year, or more if they can). I am interested in the Trust and would like some literature about it.

Name ....
(MR, MRS, MISS, ETC.)

Address ....

....

.... *Date* ....

PLEASE WRITE IN BLOCK CAPITALS AND CROSS
OUT WHAT DOES NOT APPLY

King Penguins

*

A BOOK OF DUCKS

Phyllis Barclay-Smith

K58

A well-known ornithologist has here written the first monograph on Ducks within the means of the general public. It is illustrated with sixteen attractive colour plates by Peter Shepheard and many line drawings. (3s 6d)

ACKERMANN'S CAMBRIDGE

R. Ross Williamson

K61

A History of the University of Cambridge, its Colleges, Halls and Public Buildings, was first published in 1815 by Rudolph Ackermann. This King Penguin offers for the first time a selection of twenty different scenes (in colour) from the original book. All the colleges which were existent in Ackermann's time are represented and a lively introduction has been written by Mr Ross Williamson, the topographer and architectural scholar. (4s)

LIFE IN AN ENGLISH VILLAGE

Noel Carrington and Edward Bawden

K51

This book contains sixteen colour illustrations of various scenes in village life. These were drawn by the artist directly on to lithographic zinc plates, and are therefore originals – not reproductions of drawings made on paper. Noel Carrington has introduced the pictures with a study of rural life in its relation to the general setting of to-day.

' Mr Carrington writes a brisk, shrewd, boldly generalized and comprehensive introduction to the superb drawings and lithographic plates of Mr Edward Bawden' – *The Times Educational Supplement* (2s 6d)

Wild Flowers

*

FLOWERS OF THE MEADOW

Geoffrey Grigson

K53

'Mr Grigson gives us a lively and instructive essay . . . fittingly illustrated in the coloured plates by Robin Tanner. A charming, unpretentious book.'--*The Field* (A King Penguin at 3s)

UNCOMMON WILD FLOWERS

John Hutchinson

A223

Most of the common or widely distributed wild flowers have been described and illustrated in the author's *Common Wild Flowers* (A153) and *More Common Wild Flowers* (A180). This volume deals with a selection of those that are less common, or common only in certain localities. With over 200 drawings by the author and thirty-two photographs. (A Pelican at 3s)

A companion book, now available, is Florence Ransom's *British Herbs* (A183 in the Pelican series). (1s 6d)

WILD FLOWERS OF THE CHALK

John Gilmour

K37

' It is impossible to rate too highly the sixteen colour plates. . . . No one would fail to identify a plant thus illustrated, but apart from this, each plate is a work of art. This book, small though it is, is one which every field naturalist should possess.'–*Nature* (A King Penguin at 2s 6d)

Natural History

★

BRITISH REPTILES AND AMPHIBIA

Malcolm Smith

K47

'This makes an ideal subject for a King Penguin, since there are so few species that it is possible to deal with every one of them . . . both text and illustrations are excellent and make this a very useful little popular handbook.'–*The Times Literary Supplement* (2s 6d)

SOME BRITISH BEETLES

Geoffrey Taylor

K49

'Mr Taylor writes in a lively and facetious manner of some of the most noticeable of British beetles . . . his text fits with the charming and slightly grotesque illustrations by Vere Temple. This King Penguin is a book well conceived to bring within the range of human sympathies creatures so seemingly distant and beneath our feet.'–*The Listener* (2s 6d)

SPIDERS

W. S. Bristowe

K35

'A delightful and fascinating essay to which is added a series of beautiful colour plates. Some people loathe spiders, but no one can fail to be intrigued by their weird and ingenious habits.'–*The Ex-serviceman* (A King Penguin at 2s 6d)

A BOOK OF MOSSES

Paul Richards

K57

'This charmingly produced King Penguin is an admirably lucid account of what a moss is and how it grows and reproduces itself . . . with sixteen beautifully drawn plates.'–*The Times Literary Supplement* (3s)

A New Series

THE BUILDINGS OF ENGLAND

NIKOLAUS PEVSNER

Slade Professor of Fine Art in the University of Cambridge

This series is being launched to meet a growing demand from students and travellers for more detailed information about the history and architecture of the buildings they visit. It will provide a complete and authoritative introduction to the churches, monuments, and large houses, in fact, to every structure of interest in a county, from pre-historic remains to the latest building of note, treating them village by village and town by town, and in the case of churches describing not only the exterior but also the furnishings, such as pulpits, roof-bosses, plate, and rood-screens. Each volume will contain a long general introduction to the architectural history of the county, a map, and a large section of illustrations. The first three volumes, at three shillings and sixpence each, are *Cornwall*, *Nottingham* and *Middlesex*, and *North Devon* and a volume of *London*, excluding the City and Westminster, will follow early in 1952.

*

A New Pelican

THE ESSENCE OF THE ENGLISH VILLAGE

Victor Bonham-Carter

A241

An informative survey of the English village as a place and as a community, describing its history, analysing its various elements – physical, industrial, administrative, religious and human – and outlining its probable future.